First World War
and Army of Occupation
War Diary
France, Belgium and Germany

25 DIVISION
Headquarters, Branches and Services
Royal Army Veterinary Corps
Assistant Director Veterinary Services
29 September 1915 - 28 February 1919

WO95/2232/3

The Naval & Military Press Ltd
www.nmarchive.com
Published in association with The National Archives

Published by

The Naval & Military Press Ltd

Unit 10 Ridgewood Industrial Park,

Uckfield, East Sussex,

TN22 5QE England

Tel: +44 (0) 1825 749494

www.naval-military-press.com

www.nmarchive.com

This diary has been reprinted in facsimile from the original. Any imperfections are inevitably reproduced and the quality may fall short of modern type and cartographic standards.

© Crown Copyright
Images reproduced by permission of The National Archives, London, England, 2015.

Contents

Document type	Place/Title	Date From	Date To
Heading	WO95/2232/3 Assistant Director Veterinary Services		
Heading	Asst Dir. Vety Services Sept 1915-Feb 1919		
Heading	25th Division H.Q. 25th Div Advs Vol I		
Heading	War Diary Of Major W. Ludgate, A.V.C., A.D.V.S., 25th Division. From Sept. 29th 191st To October 31st 1915 (Volume)		
War Diary	Nieppe	29/09/1915	31/10/1915
Heading	H.Q. 25th Div A.D.S. Vol. 2 Nov 15		
Heading	War Diary Of Major W. Ludgate, A.V.C., A.D.V.S., 25th Division From November 1st 1915 To November 30th 1915 Volume 2		
War Diary	Nieppe	01/11/1915	30/11/1915
Heading	A.D.S. 25th Div. Vol. 3		
Heading	War Diary Of Major W. Ludgate A.V.C., A.D.V.S., 25th Division From December 1st To December 31st 1915 Volume 3		
War Diary	Nieppe	01/12/1915	30/12/1915
Heading	25th. Div. A.D.V.S. January 1916		
Heading	War Diary Of Major W. Ludgate A.V.C., A.D.V.S., 25th Division. From January 1st 1916 To January 31st 1916 Volume 4		
War Diary	Nieppe	06/01/1916	26/01/1916
War Diary	Merris	27/01/1916	31/01/1916
Heading	25th. Div. A.D.V.S. February 1916		
Heading	War Diary Of Major W. Ludgate A.V.C., A.D.V.S., 25th Division. from February 1st 1916 to February 29th 1916 Volume 5		
War Diary	Merris	01/02/1916	17/02/1916
Heading	25th. Div. A.D.V.S. March 1916		
Heading	War Diary Of Major W. Ludgate A.V.C., A.D.V.S., 25th Division. from March 1st 1916 to March 31st 1916 Volume 6		
War Diary	Merris	01/03/1916	11/03/1916
War Diary	Pernes	12/03/1916	17/03/1916
War Diary	St Michel	18/03/1916	31/03/1916
Heading	25th. Div. A.D.V.S. April 1916		
Heading	War Diary Of Major W. Ludgate, A.V.C., A.D.V.S., 25th Division from April 1st 1916 To April 30th Volume 7		
War Diary	St Michel	01/04/1916	22/04/1916
War Diary	Camblain L'Abbe	23/04/1916	30/04/1916
Heading	25th. Div. A.D.V.S. May 1916		
War Diary	Camblain L'Abbe	01/05/1916	31/05/1916
Heading	25th. Div. A.D.V.S. June 1916		
Heading	War Diary Of Major W. Ludgate, A.V.C., A.D.V.S., 25th Division. From June 1st To June 30th 1916 Volume 8		
War Diary	Camblain L'Abbe	01/06/1916	01/06/1916
War Diary	St Michel	02/06/1916	11/06/1916
War Diary	Frohen Le Grand Domart	18/06/1916	19/06/1916

War Diary	Canaples	20/06/1916	26/06/1916
War Diary	Rubempre	27/06/1916	29/06/1916
War Diary	Contay	30/06/1916	30/06/1916
Heading	25th. Div. A.D.V.S. July 1916		
Heading	War Diary Of Major W. Ludgate, A.V.C., A.D.V.S., 25th Division From July 1st To July 31st 1916 Volume 10		
War Diary	Contay	01/07/1916	04/07/1916
War Diary	Bouzincourt	05/07/1916	07/07/1916
War Diary	Henencourt	08/07/1916	17/07/1916
War Diary	Henencourt Beauval	18/07/1916	21/07/1916
War Diary	Bus Les Artois	22/07/1916	24/07/1916
War Diary	Bertrancourt	25/07/1916	31/07/1916
Heading	25th. Div. A.D.V.S. August 1916		
Heading	War Diary Of Major W. Ludgate, A.V.C., A.D.V.S., 25th Division From Aug.1st 1916 To Aug 31st 1916 Volume 11		
War Diary	Bertrancourt	01/08/1916	06/08/1916
War Diary	Bus les Artois Acheux. Hedauville Acheux Senlis	07/08/1916	31/08/1916
Heading	25th. Div. A.D.V.S. September 1916		
Heading	War Diary Of Major W. Ludgate, A.V.C., A.D.V.S., 25th Division. From Sept1st To Sept 30th 1916 Volume 12		
War Diary	Senlis	01/09/1916	06/09/1916
War Diary	Acheux	07/09/1916	09/09/1916
War Diary	Doullens	10/09/1916	10/09/1916
War Diary	Bernaville	11/09/1916	11/09/1916
War Diary	Domqueur	12/09/1916	22/09/1916
War Diary	Doullens	25/09/1916	25/09/1916
War Diary	Acheux	26/09/1916	29/09/1916
War Diary	Bouzincourt	30/09/1916	30/09/1916
Heading	25th. Div. A.D.V.S. October 1916		
Heading	War Diary Of Major W. Ludgate, A.V.C., A.D.V.S., 25th Division. From Oct. 1st To Oct 31st 16 Volume 13		
War Diary	Bouzincourt	01/10/1916	22/10/1916
War Diary	Contay	23/10/1916	23/10/1916
War Diary	Beauval	24/10/1916	29/10/1916
War Diary	Fletre	30/10/1916	31/10/1916
Heading	25th. Div. A.D.V.S. November 1916		
Heading	War Diary Of Major W. Ludgate A.V.C., A.D.V.S., 25th Division. From Nov. 1st 1916 to Nov 30th 1916 Volume 14		
War Diary	Fletre	01/11/1916	03/11/1916
War Diary	Bailleul	04/11/1916	30/11/1916
Heading	25th. Div. A.D.V.S. December 1916		
Heading	War Diary Of Major W. Ludgate A.V.C., A.D.V.S., 25th Division From Dec 1st 1916 To Dec 31st 1916 Volume 15		
War Diary	Bailleul	01/12/1916	31/12/1916
Heading	War Diary Of Major W. Ludgate A.V.C., A.D.V.S 25th Div. From Jan 1st 1917 to Jan 31st 1917 Volume XVI		
War Diary	Bailleul	01/01/1917	31/01/1917
Heading	Intelligence Summary Of Major W. Ludgate A.V.C., A.D.V.S., 25th Division From February 1st To February 28th 1917 Volume 17		
War Diary	Bailleul	01/02/1917	28/02/1917

Heading	Intelligence Summary Of Major W. Ludgate A.V.C., A.D.V.S., 25th Division From March 1st 1917 to 31st 1917 Volume XVIII		
War Diary		01/03/1917	31/03/1917
Miscellaneous	D A G Base	12/05/1917	12/05/1917
Heading	Major W Ludgate A.V.C. ADVS 25th Division From April To April 30th 1917		
War Diary	Bailleul	01/04/1917	01/04/1917
Heading	War Diary Of Major W. Ludgate A.V.C., A.D.V.S., 25th Division From May 1st 1917 To May 31st 1917		
War Diary	Ravelsberg	00/05/1917	00/05/1917
War Diary	Ravelsberg 28.S.17 Central		
Heading	War Diary Of Major W. Ludgate, A.V.C., A.D.V.S., 25th Division From June 1st 1917 To June 30th 1917		
War Diary	Ravelsburg Camp 28.S.17 Central	01/06/1917	22/06/1917
War Diary	Bailleul	23/06/1917	23/06/1917
War Diary	Bomy	24/06/1917	30/06/1917
Heading	Major W. Ludgate A.V.C. D.A.D.V.S. 25th Division From July 1st 1917 To July 31st 1917		
War Diary	Bomy	01/07/1917	01/07/1917
War Diary	Busseboom	12/07/1917	31/07/1917
Heading	Intelligence Summary Of Major W Ludgate A. V. C., D.A.D.V.S., 25th Division from August 1st 1917 to August 31st 1917		
War Diary	Busseboom	01/08/1917	04/08/1917
War Diary	Steenvoorde (Front 17th Inst)	04/08/1917	31/08/1917
Heading	Intelligence Summary Of Major W Ludgate A.V.C., D.A.D.V.S., 25th Division From Sept 1st 1917 To Sept 30th 1917		
War Diary	Steenvoorde	01/09/1917	01/09/1917
War Diary	Reninghelst	02/09/1917	09/09/1917
War Diary	Lambeuvriere	10/09/1917	30/09/1917
Heading	Intelligence Summary Of Major W. Ludgate, A.V.C., D.A.D.V.S., 25th Division. from October 1st 1917 to October 31st 1917		
War Diary	Labeuvriere	01/10/1917	06/10/1917
War Diary	Locon	07/10/1917	31/10/1917
Heading	Intelligence Summary of Major W. Ludgate, A.V.C., D.A.D.V.S., 25th Division. from Nov 1st 1917 to Nov 30th 1917		
War Diary	Locon	01/11/1917	28/11/1917
War Diary	Greuppe	29/11/1917	30/11/1917
Heading	War Diary of Major G.D Norman, A.V.C., D.A.D.V.S., 25th Division for month of December 1917 Volume XXVII		
War Diary	Grueppe	01/12/1917	04/12/1917
War Diary	Grevillers	04/12/1917	13/12/1917
War Diary	Favreuil	14/12/1917	31/12/1917
Heading	War Diary of Major G.D Norman, A.V.C., D.A.D.V.S., 25th Division. from Jan 1st 1918 to Jan 31st 1918 Volume XXVIII		
War Diary	Favreuil	01/01/1918	31/01/1918
Heading	War Diary Of Major G.D Norman, A.V.C., D.A.D.V.S., 25th Division. from Feb 1st 1918 to Feb 28th 1918		
War Diary	Favreuil	01/02/1918	12/02/1918

War Diary	Achiet Le Petit	13/02/1918	28/02/1918
Heading	War Diary Of Major G.D Norman, A.V.C., D.A.D.V.S., 25th Division. from March 1st 1918 to March 31st 1918		
War Diary	Achiet Le Petit	01/03/1918	24/03/1918
War Diary	Puiseaux	25/03/1918	25/03/1918
War Diary	Fonquevillers Pommier	26/03/1918	27/03/1918
War Diary	Berneuil	28/03/1918	31/03/1918
Heading	War Diary Of Major G.D. Norman, A.V.C., D.A.D.V.S., 25th Division. from month of April 1918 Volume XXXI		
War Diary	Merris	01/04/1918	02/04/1918
War Diary	Ravelsberg	03/04/1918	12/04/1918
War Diary	Steenvoorde	13/04/1918	14/04/1918
War Diary	Bueschepe	15/04/1918	17/04/1918
War Diary	Boeschepe Steenvoorde	18/04/1918	21/04/1918
War Diary	Couthove Area 27. F. 21. A	21/04/1918	24/04/1918
War Diary	Couthove Chateau	25/04/1918	30/04/1918
Heading	War Diary Of Major G.D. Norman, A.V.C., D.A.D.V.S., 25th Division. from May 1st 1918 to May 31st 1918 Volume XXXII		
War Diary	Couthove Chateau	01/05/1918	03/05/1918
War Diary	Bambecque	04/05/1918	08/05/1918
War Diary	Arcis Le Ponsart	12/05/1918	22/05/1918
War Diary	Montigny	23/05/1918	26/05/1918
War Diary	Arcis Le Ponsart	27/05/1918	27/05/1918
War Diary	Gouzincourt	28/05/1918	28/05/1918
War Diary	La Chapelle	29/05/1918	30/05/1918
War Diary	Bergeres	31/05/1918	31/05/1918
Heading	War Diary Of Major G. D. Norman A.V.C., D.A.D.V.S., 25th Division. from June 1st 1918 to June 30th 1918 Volume XXXIII		
War Diary	Bergeres	01/06/1918	02/06/1918
War Diary	Etoges	03/06/1918	08/06/1918
War Diary	Allemant	09/06/1918	13/06/1918
War Diary	Pleurs	14/06/1918	25/06/1918
War Diary	Royon	28/06/1918	30/06/1918
Heading	War Diary Of Major G. D. Norman A. V. C. D.A.D.V.S. 25th Division from July 1st 1918 to July 31st 1918 Volume XXXIV		
War Diary	Aldershot	01/07/1918	31/07/1918
Heading	War Diary Of Major G. D. Norman A. V. C. D.A.D.V.S. 25th Division from aug 1st 1918 to aug 31st 1918 Volume XXXV		
War Diary	Aldershot	01/08/1918	31/08/1918
Heading	War Diary Of Major G. D. Norman A. V. C. D.A.D.V.S. 25th Division for Month of September 1918 Volume XXXVI		
Miscellaneous			
War Diary	Aldershot	01/09/1918	16/09/1918
War Diary	St Riquier	17/09/1918	25/09/1918
War Diary	Henencourt	27/09/1918	28/09/1918
War Diary	Montauban	29/09/1918	30/09/1918
Heading	War Diary Of Major G. D. Norman A. V. C. D.A.D.V.S. 25th Division for Month of October 1918 Volume XXXVII		

Miscellaneous			
War Diary	Combles	01/10/1918	02/10/1918
War Diary	Norlu	03/10/1918	03/10/1918
War Diary	St Emilie	04/10/1918	05/10/1918
War Diary	Templeux	06/10/1918	07/10/1918
War Diary	Bellicourt	08/10/1918	08/10/1918
War Diary	Fonchaux	09/10/1918	09/10/1918
War Diary	Les Troux Aux Soldats	10/10/1918	11/10/1918
War Diary	Serain	12/10/1918	18/10/1918
War Diary	Honnechy	19/10/1918	22/10/1918
War Diary	Le Cateau	23/10/1918	31/10/1918
Heading	War Diary Of Major G. D. Norman A. V. C. D.A.D.V.S. 25th Division for Month of November 1918		
War Diary	Le Cateau	01/11/1918	05/11/1918
War Diary	Landrecies	06/11/1918	12/11/1918
War Diary	Le Cateau	13/11/1918	29/11/1918
War Diary	Avesnes Lez Aubert	30/11/1918	30/11/1918
Heading	War Diary Of D.A.D.V.S. 25th Division for Month of December 1918 Volume XXXIX		
Miscellaneous			
War Diary	Avesnes Lez Aubert	01/12/1918	31/12/1918
Heading	War Diary Of Major G. D. Norman. R.A.V.C. D.A.D.V.S. 25th Division. For Month Of January 1919		
War Diary	Avesnes Lez Aubert	01/01/1919	31/01/1919
Heading	War Diary Of Major G. D. Norman R.A.V.C. D.A.V.S. 25th Division For The Month Of February 1919		
War Diary	Avesnes Lez Aubert	01/02/1919	28/02/1919

Wolas/2232

/s Assistant Director
Veterinary Services

25TH DIVISION
DIVL TROOPS

ASST DIR. VETY SERVICES
SEPT ~~OCT~~ 1915-FEB 1919

121/7431

25th Division

H.Q. 25th Div: A.D.V.S.
Vol I

Oct 15
|
Feb. '16

Confidential.

WAR DIARY
OF
MAJOR W. LUDGATE, A.V.C.,
A.D.V.S., 25TH DIVISION.

From Sept. 29th 1915.   To October 31st 1915.

(VOLUME).

Army Form C. 2118.

WAR DIARY
INTELLIGENCE SUMMARY.
(Erase heading not required.)

Instructions regarding War Diaries and Intelligence Summaries are contained in F. S. Regs., Part II. and the Staff Manual respectively. Title pages will be prepared in manuscript.

Place	Date	Hour	Summary of Events and Information	Remarks and references to Appendices
NIEPPE	29/9/15	2 p.m	Arrived here after disembarkation at HAVRE. Found billets for office etc. Interviewed D.D.V.S., 2nd Army for instructions. Found billet for Mobile Vety Section.	W.L. W.L.
"	30/9/15		Instructed O.C, Mobile Vety Section re Veterinary arrangements for evacuation & treatment of sick wounded animals, relieved V.O's & units.	W.L.
	1/10 6/10		Office & general routine work. Arranged to take V.O's in turn to visit their units with them in order that I could inspect all units once weekly.	
"	31/10/15		Recommended (1) Sending more V.O's to units softly in this district's insufficient. (2) Raised breakdowns to centre of wagon lines. RA. transport lines after units. (3) Supply of winter filling rifle in temper standing (4) That an efficient N.C.O. should always be left in charge of office in the absence of the officer in charge. Arranged instructors V.O's re Instruction of AVC Sergts in first aid dressing slight V.O's re Disposal of sick wounded animals, reporting deaths of & wounded animals F.O. units, these reports to be attached to the Unit	W.L.

Army Form C. 2118

WAR DIARY

INTELLIGENCE SUMMARY

(Erase heading not required.)

Instructions regarding War Diaries and Intelligence Summaries are contained in F.S. Regs., Part II. and the Staff Manual respectively. Title pages will be prepared in manuscript.

Place	Date	Hour	Summary of Events and Information	Remarks and references to Appendices
MEPPE			Bi-monthly Demands for Remounts as usual. Two cases of ANTHRAX occurred during the month; one in the Divl. Amn. Column at St JANS CAPPEL, & one in "A" By, 112th Bde R.F.A. at LA CRÈCHE. Instructions were issued & Preventative measures taken as circs. required.	W.1

121/7621

ans

HQ. 25 6 Bri:
ADVS.
Vol. 2

Nov. 15

CONFIDENTIAL.

WAR DIARY

OF

MAJOR W. LUDGATE, A.V.C.

A.D.V.S., 25TH DIVISION.

FROM NOVEMBER 1ST 1915 TO NOVEMBER 30TH 1915.

VOLUME 2.

WAR DIARY

INTELLIGENCE SUMMARY

Place	Date	Hour	Summary of Events and Information	Remarks and references to Appendices
NIEPPE	1915 NOV. 1st		Issued circular memo re Alteration of horse rugs by taking tuck in rug over the withers, to narrowing the neck opening & prevent the rug slipping back, galling over the horses' quarters. Until this could be done remedied was till the sgs (H.D) were therefore much too large for riders mules. Reminded that all sick horses should be taken back standing, where possible, & saddle bedding to be kept clean, that linen bandages should be covered with old brakes that have become unserviceable. Put in Orders "All rails should be brocked nails that shown over the roads for Pett Pinkedorp-Nieply, Field Firstlan wagons, etc. one a very fruitful source of lameness in the Pett Pinkedorp-Nieply. Saw all the Army Bkes + Div Am Column re transfr of F.Q.M.Ss to A.V.C. Inspected 113th Bde R.F.A. Found a large percentage of kicks the 6 horses getting loose & by breaking to lead ropes. Issued instructions re docking hind ropes. The ropes are apparently a large extent. Also tried trimming them. Found this a prevention of key. The ropes will were taken from bales of	W.I.

Army Form C. 2118.

WAR DIARY
or
INTELLIGENCE SUMMARY.
(Erase heading not required.)

Place	Date 1915	Hour	Summary of Events and Information	Remarks and references to Appendices
NIEPPE.	Nov. 2nd		Inspected 7th & 8th Bde Transport, & asked for 6 to [?] staff & me Sergeant more suitable, as there was no accommodation for office nor sleeping for [?]; changed & was billeted on 3rd inst. Reported three A.V.C. Sergeants inefficient to D.DV.S., 2nd Army, who interviewed them. On the trial considered advisable.	W.L.
	3rd.			W.L.
	4th.		Inspected 45 L.D. horses belonging to 2nd Brigading Train issued 42 & 6 R.A. Sent 3 & M.V.S. These were replaced by H.D. under instructions of D.D.R., 2nd Army.	W.L.
	5th		Class of instruction for V.O.s of this Division. Forwarded Remount Demand for this Division. Genl. in R. Stove	W.L.
	6th		Class for Shoeing Smiths at ABBEVILLE worked units to furnish men for training to complete establishment. Asked for return of order for remount horses to be forwarded to this office. Enquired what proceedings were to be taken re Transport of Ansher maintained by M.V.S.) in the event of a move, was informed that they should be handed to Ordnance for horses (which inspected 110th Bde wagon lines.	W.L.

WAR DIARY or INTELLIGENCE SUMMARY

Army Form C. 2118.

Place	Date	Hour	Summary of Events and Information	Remarks and references to Appendices
MIEPPE	1916 Nov 8th		Reported to D.D.V.S., 2nd Army arrival of Temp Capt. J.E. PORRETT, A.V.C. for duty with this Division. tasked for transfer of Temp Lieut. J.M. CROWE A.V.C. from this Div. Inspected transport of M.V.S. sent load pillows to D.D.V.S. with suggestion re alteration transport. Inspected 7th Inf/Bde Transport lines, also Pioneers, Military Mounted Police.	M
	9th		Inspected 260 mules of Divl Ammn Column; enquired to transfer 6 Arty Rgt HQ, 25th Divn Ulfa Q 705 d/7-11-15.	M
	9th		Inspected 113th Bde wagon lines, visited M.V.S. re inspected animals for evacuation.	M
	10th		Inspected Divl Cavalry 4/12 R. Bde R.F.A. Goshen Temp Capt W.G. STEDMAN, AV asked "B" Branch D.H.Q. to recommend road for M.T. train for duty of the Pack. for M.C. Engineers re wagon lines. Boots obtained and issued.	M
	11th		Inspected 113th Bde wagon lines; M.V.S. he inspected cures of mange in 113th B.A.C. took scrapings examined microscopically; negative result.	M
	12th		Inspected sick horses for evacuation to Base at M.V.S. Held class of instruction for V.O's.	M

Army Form C. 2118.

WAR DIARY
INTELLIGENCE SUMMARY.
(Erase heading not required.)

Instructions regarding War Diaries and Intelligence Summaries are contained in F.S. Regs., Part II and the Staff Manual respectively. Title pages will be prepared in manuscript.

Place	Date	Hour	Summary of Events and Information	Remarks and references to Appendices
NIEPPE	Nov 13th		Distributed Permits that arrived for the Divn to the differentiates. Inspected wagon lines of 110th Bde R.F.A. Reported departure of Lieut. J.M. CROWE A.V.C. for duty with No 4. Veterinary Hospital, C.M.A.I.S. Checked Weekly Report of Sick and Lame. (A.F. A 2000).	W⌐
	14th		Inspected wagon lines of 112th Bde R.F.A, Pioneers, 7th Inf Bde & 21st Signal Coy.	W⌐
	15th		Inspected animals for evacuation. Div Cavalry asked for D.R.O. re they not to be allowed to purchase forage which seems inadvisable. Enquiries from Divl. Supply of forage from Regimental Officers to replace the 5 lbs for H.D. or 2 lbs for L.D. of hay about issued & found that very few units were being supplied. Reported this to A.A. and Q.M.G.	W⌐
	16th		Recommended that Sgt. DUMBRILL, A.V.C. be transferred from No 1 Sect. to No 2 Section of Divl Amm Column as he does not get on well with O.C. this transfer to replace Sgt. G. ILLIAMS, A.V.C. who has been transferred 6 days ind. Corps that F.Q.M.S. SWEETONED be transferred from Sgts. Divl Amn Column to No 1 Section to act for Sergeant DUMBRILL, A.V.C.	W⌐

WAR DIARY
or
INTELLIGENCE SUMMARY
(Erase heading not required.)

Army Form C. 2118.

Place	Date 1915	Hour	Summary of Events and Information	Remarks and references to Appendices
NIEPPE	Nov. 17th		Inspected 112 & 73rd R.F.A. & 73rd Bde Army & lost 110th & 113th Bde R.F.A. Recommend wagon lines of 110th & 113th Bde for change to be slushy so animals were standing in mud over the hocks. Shoes were bad. Shoeing of 113th B.A.C. required attention (feet too long). Arrived at Neppe & F.O.C.	WH
"	18th		Attended B.S.R., 2nd Army & Inspection of units of this Divn.	WL
"	19th		Inspected Transport lines of 74th, 75th, 76th Bdes & animals for evacuation at M.V.S. Took scraping from suspected case of mange in 74th Bde for examination by lice eggs detected — ordered treatment.	WL WL
"	20th		Inspected animals for evacuation at railhead. Inspected 110th Bde wagon lines & R.E. Transport lines.	WL
"	21st		Inspected 112th Bde wagon lines Pioneers.	WL
"	22nd		Inspected Divl Train & 2nd Bridging Train.	WL
"	23rd		Inspected Divl Ammn Column.	WL
"	26th		Inspected Remt. Gen. proposed for casting with D.R. 2nd Army for this Divn. Inspected animals for evacuation with V.S. Class & instructor for Vety Officers. NOTE: Frostbite prevalent in this Divn during the first week. Recommended rubbing extremities with Wakefield's Castor Oil to prevent this. Sent written instructions to Q'B'ands to be attached to units. Preventive line measures adopted to limit cracked heels, mud fever, frostbite, rope galls or kicks.	WL
"	27th		Inspected R.E. Coys, visited Remounts to units of this Divn.	WL

WAR DIARY or **INTELLIGENCE SUMMARY.**

Army Form C. 2118.

(Erase heading not required.)

Place	Date	Hour	Summary of Events and Information	Remarks and references to Appendices
NIEPPE	Nov 28th 1915		Inspected 113th Bde R.F.A. Wagon Lines, 7th Inf Bde Transport Lines & Farriers.	W.1
"	29th		Visited M. Safety Section. Inspected animals for evacuation.	W.1
"	30th		Inspected Divl Amn Column.	W.1

A.S.M. 25th Divn.
Vol: 3

1798/121

Confidential.

War Diary
of
Major W. Ludgate, A.V.C.
A.D.V.S., 25th Division

From December 1st To December 31st. 1915.

Volume 3.

Army Form C. 2118.

WAR DIARY
INTELLIGENCE SUMMARY.
(Erase heading not required.)

Place	Date	Hour	Summary of Events and Information	Remarks and references to Appendices
NIEPPE	Dec 8/15 1st		Inspected Dual Amm Column Sr. The 2 Section attained to have been falling off in condition chiefly due to shortage of forrige or shortage. The shortage was they not in want of ration. Represented this to APM QMG, 2nd Div, PRA, ADVS Remt report to DDVS, 2nd Army. Gave DADVS re supply of horse hay nets to this Section. Recommended that the horses not of condition be put in a line by themselves to receive special attention & lilting etc.	M1
	2nd		Inspected Wagon Transport Lines of 112th Bde RFA. 74th Inf Bde asked for change of billet for M.V.S. to prevent one in being billed almost daily. This was granted.	M1
	3rd		Inspected Wagon Lines of 111th Bde RFA. 74th Inf Bde. Seen class for Vety Officers.	M1
	4th		Inspected 113th & 73rd R.F.A. & 74th Inf Bde	M1
	5th		Visited Mobile Vety Section, inspected office books returns, animals for evacuation. Checked A.F. A1006 for the Division.	M1
	6th		Office work. Inspected Divl Cavalry.	M1

Army Form C. 2118.

WAR DIARY
or
INTELLIGENCE SUMMARY.
(Erase heading not required)

Instructions regarding War Diaries and Intelligence Summaries are contained in F. S. Regs., Part II. and the Staff Manual respectively. Title pages will be prepared in manuscript.

Place	Date	Hour	Summary of Events and Information	Remarks and references to Appendices
N.E. Pozières			Started to inspection of the Divn by G.O.C. 2nd Army	W.1.
	9th		Inspected Divl Train. Took away for examination from a case of mopeded mange. Revolt-Napthine Injected. Dulcann Ointment. Found an improvement on dose of M & R solution last week. Inspected 112th-Bde-Wagon Lines, reported to H.Q., R.A. on condition of the animals of A/B/H. 112th Bde. Robo II mange, getting, & going, plenty of rations. Show animals were not isolated. To charge of forage. Mere up shortage of hay rates. Made a mark to them to enlist for rules of 110th-Bde A.C. recommended a F.C.I.M. return. They go to ket Camp Locamintes. Cases carefully Horses have a heavy poppy class of mule. Inspected 113th-Bde-Wagon Lines, been standing in mud up to over & inspected mange in the S. Lances. Took oscrapings examined microscopically. Result negative.	W.1.
	9th			W.1.

WAR DIARY

INTELLIGENCE SUMMARY

Place	Date	Hour	Summary of Events and Information	Remarks and references to Appendices
MULE PARK	10th		Inspected animals for evacuation at M.V. Sec. Checks Vety Officer's Kit.	M.
	11th		Inspected 110th Bde Wagon Lines, R.E. Coys. & Divl Signal Coy; also Syd Artillery. Reported to H.Q. R.A. that none of 110th & Bde Wagon Lines were getting the active forage for Regimental Officers. Make up shortage of hay ration.	M.
	12th		Inspected 113th Bde Wagon Lines. Checked forward weekly Returns.	M.
	13th		Inspected 7th Inf/Bde & Pioneers. Visited M.V.S. inspected animals for evacuation.	M.
	14th		Inspected Drill Train & Divl Amm Column; also C'Bty 113th Bde held to be made ready to leave the Division.	M.
	15th		Inspected Bde Amm Col. at 11 oh 7.30; "A"& "G" Battery Wagon Lines 112 & 340. Recommend of 2 lbs. of Hay per horse. Reported to H.Q. R.A. re units not receiving their horse that is about issued.	M.
	16th		Inspected M.V.S. animals for evacuation at Railhead. Examined scrapings from suspected case of Mange in one of last remounts issued to Divl Amm. Col. Result negative.	M.

WAR DIARY
or
INTELLIGENCE SUMMARY.
(Erase heading not required.)

Army Form C. 2118.

Place	Date	Hour	Summary of Events and Information	Remarks and references to Appendices
NIEPPE	Dec 17th		Office work. Inspected Mobile Vet. Sectn. Held class for Vety Officers	M
	18th		Inspected 111th Bde Wagon Lines. Reported to HQ. R.A. Re training of B.V. Rlys. were greatly trying on itan. Chiffy due to shortage of horseshoes. Saw A.D.V.S. on supply of iron & those nails. Reported on Vety Equipment to D.V.S. 2nd Army re reduction in issue of Vety Officers Chart.	M
	19th		Inspected Divl Train.	M
	20th		Inspected "B" 111th Bde RFA. Recommended extra ration (since) of carrots. Picked out 16 cases for evacuation. Chiefly due to ground recovn feels. Reported to D.V.S. 2nd Army re this inspection.	M
	21st		Inspected Wagon Lines of 113th Bde RFA.	M
	22nd		Inspected Divl Amm Column, Divl Train, Divl Cavalry.	M
	23rd		Inspected 112th Bde RFA & 74th Inf Bde.	M
	24th		Inspected M.V. Sec mainly for evacuation.	M
	25th		Inspected 111th Bde Wagon Lines. Class for Vety Officers	M
	26th		Office work	M
			Inspected Divl train. One case insipient glanders. One case suspecting of Glanders/Farcy. Invalided with Mallein Intra-venous-palpebral method. Arranged for leading of this swim	M
			W.R. Mullein ₆ Captain	M

Army Form C. 2118.

WAR DIARY
or
INTELLIGENCE SUMMARY.
(Erase heading not required.)

Instructions regarding War Diaries and Intelligence Summaries are contained in F. S. Regs., Part II and the Staff Manual respectively. Title pages will be prepared in manuscript.

Place	Date	Hour	Summary of Events and Information	Remarks and references to Appendices
MEPPE	27/12		Visited 2nd Bgde, re suspected case of Glanders. Considered to be case of Lymphangitis. Million reaction negatived to date. Visited M.V. Sec. Received orders for evacuation. Visited Purchasing Lines of 1st Bolk. Inspected sick in cross & gave instructions re preventive measures. Took receipt for evacuation.	M1
	28th		Visited Bull train. Inspected. Inspecting crew of Glanders. Million reaction negative. Inspected animals for evacuation at Rulleck. Issued Permits at Rulleck & nails of the Division.	M1
	29th		Office work. Arranging for Mellenning of this Division on Jan 11th.	M1
	30th		Proceeded on leave from Dec. 30th to Jan 8th 1916.	M1

25th. DIVISION

25th. DIV. A. D. V. S.

J A N U A R Y   1 9 1 6.

Confidential.

War Diary
of

Major W. Redgate, A.V.C.,

A.D.V.S., 25th Division.

From January 1st 1916 To January 31st 1916.

Volume 4.

Army Form C. 2118.

WAR DIARY
INTELLIGENCE SUMMARY.
(Erase heading not required.)

Place	Date 1916 JAN	Hour	Summary of Events and Information	Remarks and references to Appendices
NEPPE.	6th 7th		Returned from leave England. Arranged Programme for malleinisation of Arty, 2nd Division 13th Cavalry. Issued rubber syringes to V.O.S. & instructed them as to procedure to be adopted	WL WL
	8th		Class of instruction on Intra-dermal Palpebral Test; demonstration of test given by D.D.V.S, 2nd Army.	WL
	9th to 16th		Inspected reactions & made notes of animals giving doubtful reactions for re-testing; positive reactions of above units on 16th. NIL. Completing malleinisation	WL
	17th to 23rd			WL
	24th		On sick list with bronchitis	WL
	25th		Inspected wagon lines of 112th Bde R.F.A. Transport lines of 74th Inf Bde. & also animals for evacuation at Mob.Vet.Section. Inspected suspected examination of scrapings in 2nd R. Irish Rifles. Microscopical reported in A' Bty. 112 Bde. Ordered it to be evacuated by Mob.Vet.Section	WL WL
	26th		is suffering from Mange; gave directions for preventive measures to be adopted. Inspected 110th Bde wagon lines. Office work.	WL
MERRIS.	27th		Moved into Rest Billets at MERRIS.	WL

WAR DIARY
or
INTELLIGENCE SUMMARY.
(Erase heading not required.)

Army Form C. 2118.

(2)

Place	Date 1916 Jan	Hour	Summary of Events and Information	Remarks and references to Appendices
MERRIS.	28th		Visited billet occupied by Mob. Vet. Section; find it unsuitable in inventory, insufficient accomodation. Represented this to Divl. HdQrs. that the billet changed to one more suitable. One case of skin disease reported in 200 Coy A.S.C.; inspected this animal. Indented vaccination by Mobile Vet Section as suffering from mange. Inspected all animals of the above unit found few rifle suspicious cases, which were isolated with remainder; give directions for preventive measure to be adopted. Inspected to other companies of the Divl Train. Posted V.Os. to units in new area.	W2
	29th		Inspected 111 H.T. Bde R.F.A. Wagon lines	W2
	30th		Inspected 200 & Col A.S.C. & Ed Amblees.	W2
	31st		Inspected Wagon Lines of Divl Am Column TH.A.Vet. Section.	

25th. DIVISION

25th. DIV. A. D. V. S.

FEBRUARY 1916.

Confidential.

War Diary

of

Major W. Ludgate, A.V.C.

A.D.V.S., 25th Division.

From February 1st 1916 to February 29th 1916.

Volume 5.

WAR DIARY or **INTELLIGENCE SUMMARY**

Army Form C. 2118.

Place	Date	Hour	Summary of Events and Information	Remarks and references to Appendices
MERRIS	FEB. 1916 1st		Inspected 112th Bde R.F.A. Wagon Lines. Found no case or suspicion of mumps. Treated isolation, dressing etc. further report from V.O. Found 3 horses affected with lice in "A" Bty; gave necessary instructions for treatment. Looked for further report. Inspected 200 Coy A.S.C. Ordered a case of mumps to be sent to M.V.S. also one from 198th Coy A.S.C.	M.L.
	2nd		Inspected 110th R.M. Wagon Lines. 199th Coy A.S.C.	M.L.
	3rd		Inspected 113th Bde Wagon Lines. Found two cases of mumps in "B" Bty; sent these to M.V.S. for evacuation. Visited 4 more suspicious cases for treatment. Reported outbreak to A.D.C. R.A. Gave directions for preventive measures to be taken. Saw S.S.O. re supply of quicklime, sulphur & paraffin oil. M.A.D.S. re supply of horse clippers to this unit.	M.L.
	4th		Inspected Transport Lines of 7th Inf. Bde. Found no case or suspicion of mumps in 1st Wilts; sent to M.V.S. for treatment. Ordered two isolated clipped horses to be carried out. Found prevention stable where the former had a horse affected with mumps, but in at hands. Ordered men's kits to be disinfected. Reported A.D.M.S.	M.L.

Army Form C. 2118.

WAR DIARY
or
INTELLIGENCE SUMMARY.

(Erase heading not required.)

Place	Date	Hour	Summary of Events and Information	Remarks and references to Appendices
NERRIS	FEB 5th		Inspected Dis. Train; wkshops; report & return sent in	M1
	6th		Inspected DAC; found no case suspicious of mange in No3 Section, rest of M.V.S for further prevention treatment. Took scrapings; result negative.	M1
	7th		Inspected Transport Lines of 75th & 9th Bde; found no one suspicious of mange in 11th Cheshires; sent to M.V.S. for examination. Scabied stores rope from clinical symptoms. Gave necessary orders re preventive measures.	M1
	8th		Inspected Dis. Arty. Inspected animals to evacuate at M.V.S. Gave instructions for preparation of Calcium Sulphide solution; sulphur & nicotine wash obtained locally	M1
	9th		Inspected above units that had mange cases. also Scenery	M1
	10th		Inspected 2nd Unplace (7th, 8th & 9th), 1st and 2 cases suspicious of mange in 7th & 8th Unplace, very slightly affected; sent to M.V.S for treatment. Inoculants at open trenches at unit lines. Inspected Signal Coy. Shoeing defective; shop to be set up. Inspected horses above BHQ. Signalled Co'd it.	M1
	11th	hrs	Office work & return. Inspected HQ, 7th Bde & incoming & attached to M.V.S, 2nd army	M1
			Paralysis cases. Wrote clinical report on	M1

2353 Wt. W2544/1454 700,000 5/15 D.D.& L. A.D.S.S/Forms/C. 2118.

Army Form C. 2118.

WAR DIARY
or
INTELLIGENCE SUMMARY.

(Erase heading not required.)

(3)

Instructions regarding War Diaries and Intelligence Summaries are contained in F. S. Regs., Part II. and the Staff Manual respectively. Title pages will be prepared in manuscript.

Place	Date	Hour	Summary of Events and Information	Remarks and references to Appendices
MERRIS	Feb 12th		Inspected animals of MVS for evacuation	WL
	13/11/44		Inspected those units which had cases of mange; no further cases occurred. Arrangements for continuing relieving Svn in 16th history:- 39th Bde. 3rd Anglesey Engineer office book reports.	WL
	15th 16th & 9th		Inspecting receiving stations units, relieving of which were completed on 29th inst.	WL
	17th		Attended SDSR's inspection of transport of 74th & 7th Inf/Bdes.	WL

2353 Wt. W2544/1454 700,000 5/15 D. D. & L. A.D.S.S./Forms/C. 2118.

25th. DIVISION.

25th. DIV. A. D. V. S.

MARCH 1916.

ADVS
25 Div
Vol 6

Confidential

War Diary
of

Major W. Eagate, A.V.C.

A.D.V.S., 25th Division.

From March 1st 1916 To March 31st 1916

Volume 6.

Army Form C. 2118.

WAR DIARY
or
INTELLIGENCE SUMMARY.
(Erase heading not required.)

Instructions regarding War Diaries and Intelligence Summaries are contained in F. S. Regs., Part II. and the Staff Manual respectively. Title pages will be prepared in manuscript.

Place	Date	Hour	Summary of Events and Information	Remarks and references to Appendices
MERRIS.	MARCH 1916 1st		Inspected 115th Bde. R.F.A. Wagon Lines. Found four cases that had been isolated effected with MANGE. These were sent to Mob. Vet. Section for evacuation. Gave necessary instructions for preventive measures to be adopted. Recommended hired as an extra for twenty animals of B/A/C which were falling off in condition. Advised hire to be mixed with its oats rather than to nosebag in order to prevent wastage from oats falling out of nosebag when the animals fed their feeds.	WR
	2d.		Inspected 113th Bde. R.F.A. Wagon Lines. In "C"/B/Ty the shoeing was behind hand. I found an enquiry had been held, only one shoeing-smith was now in trouping. Reported this to Bde. & Ithesny promptly arranged for A/Bty/Bde to help them out & for men to be sent there for training so this Bty is its full Farriery establishment.	WR
	3rd		Independent Meller Returns for the Division. Weekly conference for V.O.s. Gave further instructions. D/S. Div. C. Corps received forms retiring animals retained on lines. Arranged for evacuation form from the Div. as hindered others to move.	WR
	4th		Inspected A/D. Vet. Section animals for evacuation. Offices work Return.	WR
	5th		Inspected 111th Bde. R.F.A. Wagon Lines. A/Bty animals generally in many for condition. Send Lieut Ash, were not improving for want of water. Reported this to Brig. & steps were taken to make buckets to be used, when water troughs were not available.	WR

WAR DIARY
INTELLIGENCE SUMMARY
(Erase heading not required.)

Army Form C. 2118.

Place	Date	Hour	Summary of Events and Information	Remarks and references to Appendices
MERRIS.	March 6th		Inspected Dvl Sig'nl Coy. The charge of the unit which std reported has effectively is much improved. Inspected transport lines of 7th If Bde, found all animals in good condition	MR
	7th		Inspected 7th Vet. Section. Made arrangements in connection with coming march re Vet charge of units	MR
	8th		Inspected Tpt. transport of 74th Bde; found animals in good condition	MR
	9th		Inspected Sick horses; animals in good condition. Forwarded nullein + syringes to DADVS; 1st and Army. Packed office Kits ready at 6pm to go on	MR
	10th		Marched to BUSNES	MR
	11th		Continued march to PERNES.	MR
PERNES	12th		Arrived at PERNES. Inspected 110th Bde R.F.A, 74th Inf Bde + 99 bty A.S.C. The casualties during march recommended great care to be kept above point of shoulder to prevent chafing in 74th Bde. Admitted two cases of exhaustion from A. 110th Bde R.F.A. now at sick farm 7th Fd Amb & to 7th Vet Section	MR
	13th		Went round new area & booked billets for M.V.S. office etc. Recommended to "Branch" that all animals should be sprinkled to fr. prior until stables occupied by animals of Denth Cavalry had been thoroughly disinfected & approved by V.O's in charge of units. Bde orders published re above.	MR

WAR DIARY or INTELLIGENCE SUMMARY

Army Form C. 2118.

Place	Date	Hour	Summary of Events and Information	Remarks and references to Appendices
PERNES	March 1916 14th		Office work, reports, returns.	WL
"	15th			WL
"	16th		Wrote report re proposals for effecting a saving in the employ working parties that came under my observation today. Journey to DSVS Army & HQ. Rein. Issued instructions re disinfection of buildings.	WL
"	17th		Moved from PERNES to ST MICHEL	WL
ST MICHEL	18th		Allotted M.O. to units in new area. Out making enqs at St MICHEL out of which 6 British troops managed for disinfecting of same. Also all stabling but — which still [?] accommodation of crew of Flanders & Murps in tent. Send Emg, reported to me by D.S.V.S. Third Army	WL
"	19th		Office general routine work. Inspected D.A.C. All animals picked out in [?]. Admitted one case of mange of No 1. Section to M.V.S.. Rect II & practice evolved at unit lines. Gave instructions re drying and preservative measures; 42 animals out of condition put on same for [?] & inspected	WL
"	20th		Inspected 111 H.B.A.C. RFA Major Lines. Also Transport of 75 K.S.A. Bde.	WL
"	21st		Inspected Mob. Vet. Section. running. Sent one case of [?] of mange [?] through Rapolit Rat & M.V.S. for treatment.	WL
"	22nd		Arranged for nailing of H.T. 106 Coys R.E. Inspected the animals. Rebooked sick animals of this [?] Ext. Syd Cavalry, all animals picked out, making good progress.	WL
"	23rd		Inspected 112 K.B.L. Condition of animals much improved since my last inspection.	WL

Army Form C. 2118.

WAR DIARY
INTELLIGENCE SUMMARY
(Erase heading not required.)

Place	Date	Hour	Summary of Events and Information	Remarks and references to Appendices
ST MICHEL	MARCH 1916 24th		Office work. Weekly conference of V.Os.	WL
	25th 26th		On sick list	WL
	27th		Inspected D.A.C. 17 for animals of No 1 Section falling off in condition. picked out 14 animals the rest of M.T.S. for evacuation	WL
	28th		Inspected 113 Bde R.F.A. found animals of "C"By falling off in condition; picked out 10 for evacuation.	WL
	29th		Inspected 110th Bde R.F.A. picked out 17 animals for evacuation which had lost condition	WL
	30th		Inspected 114th Bde R.F.A. animals of B.A.C. & "C"By falling off in condition, sent 18 animals for evacuation	WL
	31st		Wrote reports to "Q", H.Q. 25th Divn, A.D.V.S., Obg Army pointed out R.F.A. batteries B.A.C.s in which wastage was high. reasons to reduce casualties. Chief causes of debility were ① Shortage of oats & hay. ② Inferior quality. ③ heavy condition ④ Rebit without proper ⑤ horse rugs ⑥ animals made to cast long & muddy standings ⑦ defective conformation ⑧ Infective animals kept at a distance of water ⑨ those stock-shortness experience & feeling muddling and stable management.	WL

25th. DIVISION

25th. DIV. A. D. V. S.

APRIL 1916.

A.D.V.S. 25D
vol. 7

Confidential.

War Diary

of

Major W. Ludgate M.C. A.D.V.S., 25th Divn.

From April 1st 1916 to April 30th.

Volume 7.

WAR DIARY
INTELLIGENCE SUMMARY
(Erase heading not required.)

Army Form C. 2118.

Place	Date	Hour	Summary of Events and Information	Remarks and references to Appendices
ST MICHEL	APRIL 1916 1st to 4th		Inspected 4 Army Bdes RFA & DAC. Picked out animals showing bad of condition that then on separate report. Recommended extra diet, rest grazing as much as possible along side roads, all in firm condition. Recommended for evacuation as soon as possible reported Batteries rendering D.A.C. in which most sick were found to D.D.V.S. Third Army & Divn. Wrote report stating reasons for bad of condition suggestions to prevent wastage from this cause.	WL
"	5-13		On leave	WL
"	14		Inspected 111th Bde RFA with DDVS Third Army. Inspected 6 animals thirty animals of Bde & A/B4 looking well, those of C/B4 improving. They are deficient in the Bde. Inch conference of V.O.s. Office work & Returns	WL
"	15		Inspected DAC animals of 101 Bde, all in poor condition. Sections 2&3 looking well. Inspected 111th Bde RFA. A & B Batteries looking well. C By has about 50 animals in poor condition. & B/14 20. B.A.C. animals in poor condition sent 4 & 5 M.V.S. for evacuation. Bits very poor, small light thirty York animals recommended team & 25th Divn "D"	WL
"	16		Inspected 110th Bde Negro Lines & Divl Cavalry. Both looking well. Inspected 201 Gl. A.S.C. My 20 animals in this unit in low condition.	WL
"	17		Lectured at Third Army Arty School & inspected the animals.	WL
"	18		Inspected animals of 112th Bde RFA at 46th Divl Area with DDVS, Third Army. Animals of A/B4 in poor condition. Picked out 40 for special dieting recommended & for evacuation. Animals of B/B4 in fair condition.	WL
"	19.		Office. Usual Routine work. Inspected animals for evacuation at MVS, chiefly for debility. Inspected Divl Units. Evacuated 2 for debility from Signal Coy.	WL

WAR DIARY

INTELLIGENCE SUMMARY

Army Form C. 2118.

Place	Date	Hour	Summary of Events and Information	Remarks and references to Appendices
ST MICHEL	April 20		Inspected DAC. Animals of No 1 Sec. improving in condition. They pass quickly into mud.	M.L
"	21		Inspected 111 Bde RFA. Animals of CBH & BAC improving. Weekly Conference of V.Os. Office Returns.	M.L
"	22		Inspected DAC. 112 & 113 Bde RFA Amm Col. Animals of No 1 Sec DAC gradually improving. 112 Bde horses well. Inspected animals for evacuation at M.V.S. Left 8 animals unfit for work with M.V.S. 46 Divn for evacuation. Marched to CAMBLAIN L'ABBE.	M.L
CAMBLAIN L'ABBE	23			
"	24		Allotted 6 V.Os to units in new area. Inspected Divl Train Cavalry. All animals looking well.	M.L
"	25		Inspected 111th Bde. Not sufficient water troughs. Reported this to H.Qrs. Divn. "Q". Had more supplied. Inspected 112 & 113 Bde RFA. Animals of A.B.H. & H.B. in poor condition.	M.L
"	26		Inspected 110 & 111 Bde RFA. All animals in good condition. Inspected 3 Buch Cy RE & 75 Fd Amb &c looking well. Inspected Transport lines of 75 & 74 I.Bde. Animals of Machine Gun Cy very improved, fed off ground. Have hypothyrets not in use. Reported this to H.Qrs. Divn "Q".	M.L
"	27		Inspected 30 LDs sent by No 1 Sec DAC to 113 Bde RFA. Found 15 to be unsuitable & for deblystyrent & M.V.S. 10 too small & lightskinned for these to be returned & replaced. Wrote report to "Q" re this. Inspected transport animals of 74 Inf Bde. All looking well. Inspected animals of 76 Inf Bde. All looking well. Sent as charge to M.V.S for debility.	M.L

Army Form C. 2118.

WAR DIARY

INTELLIGENCE SUMMARY.

(Erase heading not required.)

Place	Date April 1916	Hour	Summary of Events and Information	Remarks and references to Appendices
CAMBLAIN L'ABBE	27		Inspected 113th Bde. Animals all looking well. Very few cases of injuries in above units.	M.R.
"	28.		Inspected animals for evacuation at M.V.S. Weekly Conference of Vety. Officers.	M.R.
"	29		Inspected transport animals of 75th Inf. Bde. S.Borders, 11th Cheshires, 8th K.O.s.B. all looking well, but shoeing requires attention. Tubs for gun require slightly especially in 8 Cheshires, 8th K.O.s.B. also. Pointed this out to the Transport Officer. Sheep defenders what was required. Sheep no mule properly shod & feet taken down in an example. Inspected 112th Bde. R.F.A. Animals in B. & D. Batteries B.A.C. looking well. About 8 to 10 animals in above listed N.O.K. recommend listed for base. Animals of A. Bty slightly improving.	M.R.
"	30		Inspected C. & D. Batteries B.A.C. of 112th B.A. with D.D.V.S, 3rd Army. Inspected 113th Bde. R.F.A. remounted one case of open joint took to 6 M.V.S. All the batteries B.A.C. looking well. 'D' Bty had no big kits in mar, Reported this to A.C. 13 Bde.	M.R.

25th. DIVISION

25th. DIV. A. D. V. S.

MAY 1916.

WAR DIARY or INTELLIGENCE SUMMARY

Army Form C. 2118

ADVS 25 Div

Place	Date 1916 May	Hour	Summary of Events and Information	Remarks and references to Appendices
CAMBLAIN L'ABBÉ	1st		Inspected 7th Inf Bde Transport, 10th Cheshires, shoeing requires attention. Mules feet to long. Shoes to big. At 1st M.G. Coy shoeing also behind hand, rely on cheap smith, have spare men in training. Condition of animals good. Returned shoeing to Supt Bde. Visited M.V.S, inspected animals for evacuation.	W.L.
"	2nd		Inspected 2 + 3 sec DAC. Condition of animals good; about 20 mules with slight galls - collar galls (last joined remts). Had three animals picked nt, gave orders for treatment, poking of gunner front lines, & to keep well above point of shoulder.	W.L.
"	3rd		Inspected 111 H Bde RFA. "B" Bty, 36 horses picked nt for not pleasid shoeing. Going etc "D" Bty 20 animals picked nt. "C" Bty animals improving gradually. "A" Bty all animals looking well.	W.L.
"	4th		Inspected w/ Sec D.A.C. to 20 animals placed in tin line at last inspection, for extra diet, etc. are picking up well. Inspected 2nd Cavalry, animals looking well. Inspected 14th M.G. Coy, shoeing defective, mules feet much too long, had one mule shod as an example, reported above fact to Sup. Bde.	W.L.
"	5th		Inspected 113 H Bde RFA; all animals looking well. Weekly conference for V.O.	W.L.
"	6th		Inspected A & B L.N. Bancs. Reports returned.	W.L.
"	7th		Inspected 7th Inf Bde: animals looking well but shoeing requires attention in 9th Devillers 7 & 7 6+7. 2 Inflers all animals looking well.	W.L.
"	8th		Inspected 112 H Bde R.F.A. Animals of "A" Bty gradually improving. "B" "C" & "D" R.F.A. animals looking in fair condition. Inspected animals for evacuation at M.V.S. Chiefly for debility.	W.L.
"	9th		Inspected 110 H Bde R.F.A., animals in good condition. Inspected 27 H Bde M.G. Coy animals improved, grooming, general management better. Shoeing of battery mules improved since last inspection, condition of animals good.	W.L.

WAR DIARY / INTELLIGENCE SUMMARY

Army Form C. 2118.

Place	Date 1916 MAY	Hour	Summary of Events and Information	Remarks and references to Appendices
OMBLAIN L'ABBAYE	9th		Inspected 105, 106 & 130 Bde Amm Cols R.F.A. Condition & general management good. Inspected 7th Bde M.G.Coy, showing much improved. Inspected M.V.S. where animals cared & fit for work. Inspected Sub Convoy before leaving this Divn & join V Corps, all animals working well. Inspected 10th & 11th Bde R.F.A., condition of animals good. Inspected 7th Inf Bde.	M/L
"	10th 11th		All draught animals looking well; no sick. Shoeing of M.G. Coy much improved. Inspected 110th Bde R.F.A. B.Bty animals badly groomed, slovenly condition, one 5 tin animal. No reply. Reported this to H.Q. R.F.A. R.S.O. of animals looking well also R.A.C. Inspects 5th Bty R.F.A. "A" & "B" Bty animals being well also R.A.C. Inspects Shifty ability cases from R.H. Arty & bad conformation.	M/L
"	12th 13th		Inspected D.A.C. No 2 & 3 reco animals looking well, one two cases suspicions of mange from the regt & Bdes & condition. No 1 Sec 10 rgs in reserve.	M/L
"	14th		Re-inspected No 3 Section + Bde 6 condition. Team Weekly Conference for V.O.t weekly Reports. Somewhat different reports on Critters asked Conference with Allied some hieves of D.A.V.S.	M/L
"	15th to 19th		Inspected 111th Bde R.F.A. animals picked out that in the lines improving with special dieting. Inspected animals under treatment at M.V.S. Examined all animals in Arty Bdes & very suspicious of Inf Arty picked out all animals of poor conformation had there for transfer from the Division. Weekly Conference for V.O.t weekly Reports.	M/L
	20th to 23rd		Inspected 111th Bde R.F.A. Examined 2 cases suspicions of mange from 'B' Bty Re-inspected Arty Bdes, all animals now looking well - not complete & sharp & animals very much improved since weeding-out completed.	M/L
	24th		Inspected Sub Drain Inv 1 & 2 Corps looking well, animals well groomed, cared for. No 3 Coy picked out 2 cases suspicions of mange for keeping isolation in civil lines.	M/L

WAR DIARY
INTELLIGENCE SUMMARY

(Erase heading not required.)

(3)

Army Form C. 2118.

Place	Date 1916 May	Hour	Summary of Events and Information	Remarks and references to Appendices
CAMBLAIN L'ABBÉ	24th (cont)		to Cav. Picked out 2 cases suspicious of mange sent to M.V.S. signed recommendation for preventive measures to be adopted. All other animals looking well in this Bde.	NL
"	25th		Inspected 113th Bde RFA. Animals in very good condition.	NL
"	26th		Weekly conference for V.Os. Weekly Reports. Returns. Inspected animals for evacuation at M.V.S.	NL
"	27th		Inspected Nos 1, 2, 3 & 60 D.A.C. Picked out 4 cases suspicious of mange in 1st Section for survey at unit line. These animals had previously been treated for lice. All animals from Bdes where there were difficult to keep in condition owing to conformation which could not be disposed of or unfit animals have been transferred to D.A.C. consequently this unit has not got generally speaking, and a good stamp or to Bdes.	NL
"	28th		Inspected the 4 Army Bde with A.A.D.M.G. All looking well. Inspected 38 animals rejected by 51st Divn with D.S.R. & D.V.S. 3rd Army, 31 of which were then accepted, remaining were sent to ABBEVILLE.	NL
"	29th		Office work. Returns & Reports. Inspected Pioneers. Cavalry & animals good.	NL
"	30th		Being present. Inspected animals at M.V.S. for evacuation. Both grazings, 1 H.D. which were in use are finished and is for trench in turnpike; Claytron 2½"x5" & "112 H.Sho for unfitting R.F.A. All animals looking well; showing now good. Arranged for transport of unfitting R/s 51st Divn Arthur to M.G. Coys.	NL
"	31st		Inspected Divl. Train Kent 2 Coys which were inches in 3 Coy suspicious of mange & H.V.S. for evacuation. All animals looking well.	NL

25th. DIVISION

25th. DIV. A. D. V. S.

JUNE 1916.

CONFIDENTIAL.

WAR DIARY

OF

MAJOR W. LUDGATE, A.V.C.,

A.D.V.S., 25TH DIVISION.

FROM JUNE 1ST TO JUNE 30TH
1916.

VOLUME 8.

WAR DIARY
INTELLIGENCE SUMMARY
(Erase heading not required.)

Army Form C. 2118.

Instructions regarding War Diaries and Intelligence Summaries are contained in F.S. Regs., Part II. and the Staff Manual respectively. Title pages will be prepared in manuscript.

Place	Date JUNE 1916	Hour	Summary of Events and Information	Remarks and references to Appendices
CAMBLAIN L'ABBÉ	1st.		Inspected A.A.C. Several animals show condition to throw suspicion of mange but slight, not able for treatment. No return of animals suspicious of mange at M.V.S. on evacuation of affected. Thanked to Reserve Area.	W.L.
ST MICHEL	2nd.		Office work. Wrote weekly reports. returns.	W.L.
"	3rd.		Inspected M.V.S. animals for evacuation. Inspected train. Picked out two cases suspicious of mange. Sent to M.V.S. Inspected animals of R.E. Coys. looking well, but two suspect of little recovered standing in mud, huts to frequently, hopeless that be able to get especially the hind legs dry.	W.L.
"	4th		Inspected Army Bdes and 3 cases suspicious of mange (no. 10) are defective sick of they receiving sufficient, lunging etc. before returning to site of lines sent to M.V.S. to ascertain. Animals in some of the batteries have their off in conditions and no wet weather turn-in, poor at grooming small order close to run being attended, recommended that grass be fed in small quantities, not more than 4 to 5 lbs mixed with Ration Indian.	W.L.
"	5th		Office work. Reports. Inspected animals for evacuation at M.V.S. chiefly mange.	W.L.
"	6th		Office work. Reserve Park not yet... animals sound about extremities.	W.L.
"	7th		Inspected M.V.S. equipment, office books etc.	W.L.
"	8th		Inspected S.A.F. Transport all looking well, shoeing much improved.	W.L.
"	9th		Inspected Permits, office note, Returns & Reports. Arranged for inspection of Chico-Irigoyen horses.	W.L.
"	10th		Inspected S.A.C. All animals looking well. Inspected S.A.C. that animals that were inoculated suspicious mange returned.	W.L.

2353 Wt. W2544/1454 700,000 5/15 D. D. & L. A.D.S.S./Forms/C. 2118

WAR DIARY
INTELLIGENCE SUMMARY

Army Form C. 2118.

Place	Date	Hour	Summary of Events and Information	Remarks and references to Appendices
ST MICHEL	JUNE 11th to 18th		Malleining 7 NCOs C/10th Bde RFA in one case of clinical glanders apprehended each night. Full reports on daily action taken. Final report on T.A.B.S.N.S., Third Army. These reports dealt with the following headings:—	/WL
FOSSEN LE GRAND				
DOMART			1. History of outbreak. 2. Measures adopted to control same. 3. Mallein test. 4. Source of infection. 5. Sanitary measures adopted. 6. Report of all Transfers (including sick) to other units in mobile division.	
	19th		Interviewed D.D.V.S., Fourth Army re arrangements for evacuation during operations. Inspection 7th & 8th Bde Chilly. 6 platoons 4/10th had been away from Smp for 3 weeks; malleining of 110 & 111 Bdes RFA Ribemont (bounded R.T.V.S. 3rd Army)	/WL
CANAPLES	20th to 26th		Marched from Canaples to Rubempre. Visited V.O. 8 units. Inspected 111th Bde RFA, SAO	/WL
RUBEMPRE	27th		Visited various units. One hid. in few cases of mange.	/WL
"	28th		Inspected Shivers & Stamplers, animals looking well.	/WL
	29th		Inspected animals for evacuation at MVS, chiefly for debility from S.A.C.	/WL
CONTAY	30th		Marched from RUBEMPRE to CONTAY. Road V.O. 8 units inspected S.A.C.	/WL

25th. DIVISION

25th. DIV. A. D. V. S.

JULY 1916.

25 July
ADVS
vol 10

— Confidential —

— War Diary —

— of —

— Major W. Ludgate, A.V.C., —

— A.D.V.S., 25th Division —

— From July 1st To July 31st —
— 1916 —

— Volume 10. —

Army Form C. 2118.

WAR DIARY
or
INTELLIGENCE SUMMARY
(Erase heading not required.)

Instructions regarding War Diaries and Intelligence Summaries are contained in F. S. Regs., Part II. and the Staff Manual respectively. Title Pages will be prepared in manuscript.

Place	Date 1916	Hour	Summary of Events and Information	Remarks and references to Appendices
CONTAY	JULY 1		Office work returns. Inspected 110R 15th RFA - A&B 15th looking well. C 15th looking poor.	WL
"	2d		Inspected animals at M.V.S. for evacuation - also for debility. Inspected 3 animals reported by V.O. as suspicious of glanders. 2 from SAC with ulcer enlarged maxillary gland rejected; one from A111th reg RFA not much suspicious on return. Cast to M.V.S. all rejected. Visit by Veterinary off. higher formation — Scarcely enough rations — Inspected all animals at M.V.S. Inspected 111th RFA - all animals looking well.	WL
"	3rd		Inspected 3 leaders picked out, are slight treated with mange on jaws. Sent it to M.V.S. for treatment. Ordered R.O. to take precautions.	WL
"	4th		Inspected 112th Bde RFA. A&B/R.H. animals thirty improvement have lost condition again. Reported this to 6" & 10" H.O. R.A. Enumerated forces to M.V.S. for debility. Put 12 in hospital conditions for special feeding in new area. Published D.R.O. giving position	WL
BOUZINCOURT			Trekked to BOUZINCOURT. Appointed V.O. to units in new area. Published D.R.O. giving position of M.V.S. Passed during station.	
"	5th		Inspected 7th Infantry transport — all looking well	WL
"	6th		Inspected 74th Infantry transport — all looking well except M.G. Cpt. & limbers.	WL
"	7th		Inspected 75th Infantry transport — all looking well	WL
"	8th		Inspected M.V.S. animals for evacuation also Sick H.Q. units. Inspected "A" Bty. 110th the animals slightly for mange — killed at night.	WL
HENENCOURT	9th		Marched to HENENCOURT. Arranged for handing over of 111th Bde RFA. RE Coys & Pioneers to Capt Howetson A.V.C who agreed in relief of Capt Bonnet, A.V.C	WL
"	9th		Inspected RE Coys & Pioneers — all looking well. Office work returns.	WL

WAR DIARY
or
INTELLIGENCE SUMMARY

Army Form C. 2118.

Place	Date 1916	Hour	Summary of Events and Information	Remarks and references to Appendices
HENENCOURT	July 10th		Inspected No 4 Sec. D.A.C - mules looking well, horses fair. Inspected D.W.C train, all animals looking well.	J.L.
"	11th		Inspected Nos 1, 2 & 3 Secs D.A.C - mules in good condition, horses fair condition. Inspected "A" 112 H. Bde. Animals again futy, reported to ts. to Lt. Col. Strover. Ordered 1/2 eye erosions of mange to apply three orders for all horses & few to be disinfected under supervision of V.O.	J.L.
"	12th		Inspected 111 H. Bde RFA looking well. Inspected 110th H. Bde RFA "B" & "D" Animals looking well. 50% of animals of "B"/111 in rather poor condition. Isolated two suspicions of mange, under observation.	J.L.
"	13th		Inspected field ambulances - all looking well. Inspected 74th & 75th Bde transport - all animals looking well. Inspected animals at M.V.S for debility mange. Inspected mules removals just received by D.A.C. Sent one case to M.V.S suspicions of mange. Also one case of abrasions. Specimen to M.V.S for mallening fluid - result negative.	J.L.
"	14th		Office work returns.	
"	15th		Inspected 114th Bde R.F.A. t' animals pt M.V.S for evacuation. Inspected animals at No 1 Coy. D.W. train reported suspicions of pharaf - suffering lymphitis.	J.L.
"	16th		Inspected "A"/112 H. Bde, growing improved remarks looking much better	J.L.
"	17th		Inspected "B"/111 H. Bde for mange. Sent one case to M.V.S, lod in orturts isolated, inspected animals of "A", "C" & "D" batteries looking well.	J.L.

WAR DIARY

INTELLIGENCE SUMMARY

(Erase heading not required.)

Army Form C. 2118.

Place	Date 1916	Hour	Summary of Events and Information	Remarks and references to Appendices
HENENCOURT	19		Inspected horse from 110th Bde tet gave doubtful reaction, this animal was destroyed. This animal gave further reaction was destroyed – military rifles in both lungs – reported to DDVS.	NL
BEAUVAL	20		Inspected DVS equipment, office books etc, animals for evacuation. Marched to BEAUVAL. 18½.	NL
"	21			NL
BUS les ARTOIS	22		Inspected 74th Inf Bde Transport – one case of mange in M.G. Coy sent to M.V.S for evacuation. Marched to Bus les ARTOIS. Appointed V.O.s to units. Weekly reports returns.	NL
"	23		Inspected B/111th Bde for mange – 7 cases very under treatment violation with slight mange in fans of suspicious cases. Inspected 110th Bde RFA. One case Pleurisy. In "A"Bty for isolation C' Batty animals in poor condition. Inspected fats. Two cases of mange in Ind Section to be evacuated at once.	NL
"	24		Inspected M.S animals for evacuation + treatment. Also 74th Inf Bde Transport + 199 Coy M.S.C. Marched to BERTRANCOURT. Appointed V.O.s to units	NL
BERTRANCOURT	25		Inspected 112 Bde RFA. Condition of animals much improved in "A""B" Btys. C's D Btys also looking well.	NL
"	26		Inspected 75th Inf Bde Transport – looking well but shoeing of 7th M.G Coy is behind hand. Animals feet much too long + shoes require removing. Only one being smith.	NL
"	27		Inspected Pioneers + 10th + 11th 7th 3d Cos R.E. all looking well.	NL

Army Form C. 2118.

WAR DIARY
or
INTELLIGENCE SUMMARY
(Erase heading not required.)

Place	Date 1916	Hour	Summary of Events and Information	Remarks and references to Appendices
BERTRANCOURT	28		Inspected M.T. personnel with D.T.O.S; Remount Army; office work & Returns. Asked "Q" to arrange for malleining of S.A.O. + 70 + 74 RFA — 50% of two batteries at a time; and if possible one section of S.A.C. at a time. 8 days to complete.	W.R.
"	29		Inspected 3rd Amblers	W.R.
"	30		Inspected 110, 111, 112 B.Coy RFA + 74 Inf Bde. Inspected 74th Bde Ammn. Col. also Small Arm Sectn of Bde Transport looking well. Shoeing of M.G. Coy requires attention. Two mules looking well; Horse in rather poor condition.	W.R.
"	31		Inspected Sick Lines, Nos 2, 3 + 4 Cos. All animals looking well. Office work & Returns.	W.R.

25th. DIVISION

25th. DIV. A. D. V. S.

AUGUST 1916.

WAR DIARY

— OF —

Major W. Ludgate, A.V.C.,

A.D.V.S., 25th Division

From Aug.1st 1916 To Aug.31st 1916

Volume 11

Army Form C. 2118.

WAR DIARY
INTELLIGENCE SUMMARY
(Erase heading not required.)

Place	Date	Hour	Summary of Events and Information	Remarks and references to Appendices
BERTRAMCOURT	Aug 1916 1st		Inspected animals for evacuation at Mob.Vet.Sec. Inspected M/R. 100th Bde Cyc.R.E. Nothing noted. Inspected 6th I.W. Borderers (Pioneers). Mule lines bad condition. Slightly neglected. Transport officer complains of quality of rats issued. Chest-thin & light.	WZ
"	2nd		Inspected 111th Bde R.F.A. All animals looking well. No mange cases. Asked for slings & camp for "B" Batty. 111 Bde R.F.A. exposure in mud duty. from wind traffic. Reported watering arrangements unsatisfactory - watering troughs provided inadequate.	WZ
"	3rd		Reports Office work. Inspected 112 Bde R.F.A. "A" Batty animals dirty & badly groomed - picked up. Mane in lines with slight mange. Told in writing. Ordered evacuation of this mule. Are already isolated as suspicious. Reported dirty condition of animals to H.Q. R.F.A. T.C.Unit. "B", "C" & "D" Batteries looking well.	WZ
"	4th		Inspected 25th.H.T.G. No 2, 3 & 4 Sections looking well - No 3 Sec had two animals under observation for mange - Sent these to M.V.S. for evacuation as mange. No 1 Sec mule looking well - Two horses in poor condition. Their teeth wanted recommended dieting on green food. Neat weekly conference for veterinary officers.	WZ
"	5th		Inspected 74th Inf Bde transport. 9th L.N.Lancs & M.G.Coy. mules being condition. To Lay rifts in one in these units. Reported this to H.Q. Bde. 11th Lancs Fus, 13th R.Rifles & 13th Cheshires looking well. Posted Capt "BRYAN, R.V.C" on his arrival from France to 110th Bde R.F.A. in relief of Capt FORREST, A.V.C. transferred as O.C., 37, Mob.Vet.Sec.	WZ

WAR DIARY
INTELLIGENCE SUMMARY

Army Form C. 2118.

Place	Date	Hour	Summary of Events and Information	Remarks and references to Appendices
BERTRANCOURT	30/6/16	B.M.	Posted Capt. JONES, RVC on his arrival from No 22 Vety Hospital in relief to Capt. FERGUSON, RVC transferred to No 22 Vety Hospital on account of ill health. to 25 L Fd Amb Train. Handed over M.V.S. to Capt FORREST RVC, checked equipment etc with him. Capt PLAYER, RVC who was commanding the unit was transferred to No 22 Veterinary Hospital under instructions from D.D.V.S., Reserve Army. Inspected two cases reported by VO to 11/2 Bde R.F.A. recovering of Peery-diagnosed as Sporadic Benign from Lymphangitis-Lymphangitis - sent to M.V.S. for evacuation.	W.R.
Bus bo Acors Acheux Hedauville Acheux Genlis	7th to 31st.		Inspected percheron mules of 25 H.T.A.C., 110, 111 Bde R.F.A. & C/75 Battn 11/2 Bde R.F.A. This comprised the mallein of the 25th Divisional Artillery since the second test for I.A.G. on 17 the Dye which units had one clinical case each. Note was these suspected reactors in field which were sent to Mob Vet Section for retesting. Reports sent to D.D.V.S., Reserve Army.	W.R.

25th. DIVISION

25th. DIV. A. D. V. S.

SEPTEMBER 1916.

Vol 12

WAR DIARY.

OF

MAJOR W. LUDGATE, A.V.C.,

A.D.V.S., 25TH DIVISION.

FROM SEPT 1ST TO SEPT 30TH 1916

VOLUME 12.

Army Form C. 2118.

WAR DIARY

INTELLIGENCE SUMMARY.

(Erase heading not required.)

Place	Date SEPT.	Hour	Summary of Events and Information	Remarks and references to Appendices
SENLIS	1st		Inspected 110th Bde R.F.A. "B"By animals are falling off in condition. Reported this to O.C. unit and made enquiries into stable management. "A"C+D"Btys looking well.	WK
"	2d		Inspected D.A.C. The 2, 3 + 4 Sections looking well. Hg Coy horses in fair condition; mules looking well. Two horses in poor condition reported to "skin line" for special dieting.	WK
"	3rd and 4th		Inspected reactors to mallein of two mules were here from D.A.C. which gave doubtful reactors at last testing of this unit. These gave negative reactions, were returned to unit. Inspected two observation cases isolated at M.V.S. from 112th Bde suspicious of symptoms. These were tested and gave negative reactions on Aug 31st. The horse showed numerous nodules in septum, rigs & forehead to small tear, firm and greyish in colour; the other congested micoid discharge in septum. Decided to keep these under observation for a further period + test. Sept 3rd. Attended conference at A.D.V.S. office at which new plans & improvements for water troughs, sulphur and lime baths in regions of Armies and new pattern nose helmets were discussed.	WK
"	5th and 6th		Inspected all animals of 112th Bde. R.F.A. particularly for glanders and mange. Had two cases sent to M.V.S. for observation with mild superficial nodules on septum from A/112th Bde which considered mine cases by spring of stable land. These were tested and gave negative reactions. Animals of this Bde are looking well, free from skin disease.	WK

Army Form C. 2118.

WAR DIARY
INTELLIGENCE SUMMARY
(Erase heading not required.)

Place	Date 1916	Hour	Summary of Events and Information	Remarks and references to Appendices
ACHEUX	SEPT 7th		Inspected 111th Bde R.F.A. All looking well. Three men skin disease Division composed much to Rostrenes. Transfered from SENLIS to ACHEUX. Inspected new billet of M.V.S. at ACHEUX and Evacuation area. To change to membrane H/F. Posted V.O.s to units. Handed over Divl Artillery (3 Bdes and D.A.C.) to H.A.V.S., 11th Division, and left three V.O.s in charge.	H/F
"	8th		Inspected Infantry Transport of 74th Bde, and 75th Inf Amblce; also 105 Fld. F.C. all looking well.	H/F
"	9th		Inspected Transport of 74th Inf Bde, 76th Inf Amblce & 106th Fd.A.R.C. The animals of the latter owing to hard work, are falling off slightly in condition, sent two animals to Evacuation to M.V.S., as feel more not debility. Remainder on fair daily intake of three and arranged for a supply of linseed for animals not in good condition in this unit.	H/F
DOULLENS	10th		Marched to DOULLENS. Posted V.Os to units. Inspected billet of M.V.S. at BEAUVAL.	H/F
BERNAVILLE	11th		Marched to BERNAVILLE. Arranged for collecting of animals left behind on line of march by M.V.S. Inspected billet of M.V.S. at BERNAVILLE.	H/F
DOMQUEUR	12th		Marched to DOMQUEUR. Inspected billet of M.V.S.	H/F
	13th		Posted V.Os to units in new area. Arranged for collection of animals left behind on line of march by M.V.S. Inspected animals for evacuation and observation at M.V.S.	H/F
"	14th		Inspected transport of 75th Inf Bde, 130 Fld.A.P.C. and 77th Inf Amblce. All looking well.	H/F

WAR DIARY

INTELLIGENCE SUMMARY.

(Erase heading not required.)

Army Form C. 2118.

(3)

Place	Date SEPT. 1916	Hour	Summary of Events and Information	Remarks and references to Appendices
DOMQUEUR	14th (G.S.)		Ordering Stanits to scrounge out from annexe troughs filled by water-cart; each kitchen having a separate trough.	HL
"	15th		Inspected 25th Div: Train, all animals looking well. Weekly reports and returns.	HL
"	16th to 21st		Carried out inspection of transport animals of the Inf. Bdes, R.E. Coys, Ambulances, and Fld. Train in Reserve area, and animals for evacuation and observation at M.V.S. Nothing of interest to report.	HL
"	22nd		Two horses from 112th Bde that were under observation were rejected cases, report on Sept. 22nd, reactions negative. One with thick congested medial discharge refusing to separate was destroyed etc and was joined. The other with nodules on L.B. and for further observation.	HL
DOULLENS	25th		Marched from DOMQUEUR to DOULLENS.	HL
ACHEUX	26th		Marched from DOULLENS to ACHEUX. Posted V.Os to units.	HL
"	27th		Inspected animals for evacuation at M.V.S.; also filled of M.V.S.	HL
"	28th		Inspected Infantry Transport and M.V.S. with AA and Q.M.G., 25th Division.	HL
"	29th		Took over veterinary arrangements from A.D.V.S., 11th Division of new area round SENLIS and BOUZINCOURT.	HL
BOUZINCOURT	30th		Travelled from ACHEUX to BOUZINCOURT. Inspected animals sent for evacuation to Mob. Vet. Section.	HL

25th. DIVISION

25th. DIV. A. D. V. S.

OCTOBER 1916.

Vol 13

CONFIDENTIAL

WAR DIARY

OF

MAJOR W. LUDGATE, A.V.C.,

A.D.V.S., 25TH DIVISION.

FROM OCT 1st 16 TO OCT 31st 16.

VOLUME 13.

WAR DIARY
INTELLIGENCE SUMMARY

Army Form C. 2118.

Place	Date	Hour	Summary of Events and Information	Remarks and references to Appendices
BOUZINCOURT	OCTOBER 1916 1st		Marched from ACHEUX to BOUZINCOURT. Inspected billet of M.V.S. at SENLIS, & animals left behind for evacuation by M.V.S. 111th Div'n, unable to march. Inspected 111th Bde R.F.A. Animals in good hardworking condition.	h/h
	2nd		Office work & general routine work. Posted V.O.s 6 units in new area. Work start for month of September. Arranged for fatigue party (six men) of T.Us from Divisional Coy to work at M.V.S. clearing up lines, digging graves etc, as M.V.S. have 6 evacuated from Corps Troops and 111th Div'l Artillery in addition to our own Divisn.	h/h
	3rd to 6th		Inspected all Divisional Artillery, which have been attacked for past three weeks to 111th Division, & sent in reports regarding condition of animals to "Q", arranged for 50 animals in poor condition to be evacuated at once for debility, replaced by horses from B.A.C.; these to be replaced by L.D. mules.	h/h
			The horses of 110th and 112th Bdes R.F.A. have fallen off very much in last three weeks distance to take ammunition to Battery positions 7 Kilos, two journeys daily, meaning 28 kilos this over very heavy going, & for last two Kilos the ground is pitted with shell holes.	h/h
			Forage for past week has been coarse, & of very poor feeding quality.	h/h
			About 30% of hay ration is wasted owing to shortage of hay nets.	h/h

Army Form C. 2118.

WAR DIARY
or
INTELLIGENCE SUMMARY

(Erase heading not required.)

Instructions regarding War Diaries and Intelligence Summaries are contained in F. S. Regs., Part II. and the Staff Manual respectively. Title Pages will be prepared in manuscript.

Place	Date October 1916	Hour	Summary of Events and Information	Remarks and references to Appendices
BOUZINCOURT	3rd to 8th (Oct)		Nothing suitable in lieu of shortage of 2 lbs of hay. Want of supervision in feeding watering.	W. W
			Forwarded report to "Q" and H.Q., 51st Artillery on each battery, giving number of animals in poor condition mentioning above faults, withing measures I considered should be adopted.	W
			There is no mange or skin disease in 51st Artillery any few cases on sick lines. These are chiefly foot cases from picked up nails.	W
	9th	a.m.	Inspected the 51st Artillery with A.A. and Q.M.G., 25th Division. Artillery. Inspected 25th D.A.C. No 1 & 2 sections (class L.D.) from condition. No 3 section, all animals in fair condition, mule in good condition. Inspected No 4 Sec., 11th D.A.C. Animals in good condition. Nine mule affected with Ringworm are in working isolation. Attended conference at D.D.V.S., Office.	W
"	10th		Inspected No 4 Sec, 25th D.A.C. All animals looking well. Office work reports	W

Army Form C. 2118.

WAR DIARY
or
INTELLIGENCE SUMMARY
(Erase heading not required.)

(3)

Place	Date	Hour	Summary of Events and Information	Remarks and references to Appendices
BOUZINCOURT	OCTOBER 1916 11th		Inspected 74th & 75th Inf. Bdes. Transport. All animals looking well. Inspected animals for evacuation at M.V.S. chiefly debility. Animals from the Infantry and Pioneer. These horses were received when taking up ammunition chiefly at Cat Dump. Very few were received in the transport lines. The 74th Bde have a total of 25 mules killed wounded in last few days.	/h
"	12th		Inspected 7th Infantry Bde. The transport animals have lost condition somewhat in last 10 days owing to the heavy work they have been doing. Inspected 113 L Bde R.F.A. of this Division which arrived yesterday were attached to 2nd Army for last four months. Found animals all in good condition — picked out three cases to be evacuated for debility only.	/h
"	13th		Re-Inspected "A" and "B" Bty.s, 110 R.Bde. with O.C. Bde. N.O. — marked animals to be evacuated on account of poor condition, as soon as the remounts which have been indented for are received. Inspected animals for evacuated at M.V.S chiefly debility, galled wounds, foot cases from harness & Mud. Office work. Weekly conference for V.O.S.	/h

WAR DIARY
INTELLIGENCE SUMMARY

Army Form C. 2118.

Place	Date OCTOBER	Hour	Summary of Events and Information	Remarks and references to Appendices
BOUZINCOURT	14th		Inspected 105th, 106th & 130th Coys R.E. and 75th, 76th and 77th Fd Amblces. All animals in good condition.	1/12
"	15th		For. monthly Remount demand for this Divn was made out & forwarded to "Q", 25th Divn. Inspected cases of Contagious Pneumonia & Anthrax sent to M.V.S. for treatment from Heavy Artillery II Corps mixed M.V.S.; Reserve Army number units from which received.	1/12
"	15th		Inspected 58th & 133rd Bde R.F.A., 11th Divn with N.O. officer v/s waggon lines, and noted animals to be evacuated for debility at once.	1/12
"	16th		Accompanied by Off. i/c D.A.C. chose horses from D.A.C. to replace evacuations to debility from Artillery Bdes. These were replaced by L.D. mules on same day:- 19 horses from No 1 Eo to "A"+"B"+"C" Bdys 110th Bde, and 32 horses from No 3 Eo to A, 13 Eo Bdys, 112th Bde R.F.A. 112th Bde R.F.A. Fifty debility cases from these Bdes were sent to M.V.S. for evacuation.	1/12
"	17th		Inspected 75th Infd Fd Amb. All animals in good condition. Inspected 58th Bde R.F.A., 11th Divn with officer v/s waggon lines noted 24 cases to be evacuated for debility.	1/12
"	18th		Inspected 59th Bde R.F.A., 11th Division with N.O.; noted cases for evacuation for debility. Inspected 87 cases at M.V.S. for evacuation — 50 debility, rest surgical chiefly fore cases from P.V.N., returned wounds.	1/12

WAR DIARY

INTELLIGENCE SUMMARY

(Erase heading not required.)

Army Form C. 2118.

Place	Date	Hour	Summary of Events and Information	Remarks and references to Appendices
BOUZINCOURT	OCTOBER 1916 19th		Inspected F.W. Train, all animals looking well; fine slight cases of Ringworm in working isolation. Sent two foot cases - P.U.N. - to M.V.S for evacuation. Office work returns. Weekly Conference for V.Os.	
"	20th		Inspected animals proposed for casting for Remount Reserve from I.f. Btles.	
"	21st		Inspected 7 slight cases of Pink Eye at 59th Bde. R.F.A., 11th Divn. Gave instructions for preventative measures to be adopted. Sent report to A.D.V.S., Reserve Army; no further cases occurred.	
" and "			Wrote notes of sufficiency in hy. rets. D., 25th Divn; not complied with. Re-inspected Arty. Btles which are now much improved from evacuation of animals in foot condition being replaced by H.A.C. Remounts. Handed over vety. arrangements to A.D.V.S. 49th Divn. as 25th Divn. are under orders to march in Reserve Area tomorrow, & up to 10th A.C.A. the line attached to 19th Divn. Arty Btles & 25th D.A.C.	
"	22nd			
CONTAY	23rd		Travelled from BOUZINCOURT to CONTAY. Inspected billet of M.V.S.	
BEAUVAL	24th		Travelled from CONTAY to BEAUVAL inspected billet of M.V.S. Posted V.Os to units giving map reference.	

WAR DIARY
INTELLIGENCE SUMMARY

Army Form C. 2118.

Place	Date	Hour	Summary of Events and Information	Remarks and references to Appendices
BEAUVAL	October 1916 25th		Office work. Rendered report to D.G. giving the numbers & causes of evacuation & deaths attributable to each unit of the Division during operations on the SOMME	/R
"	26th		Route inspection with V.O. of 2nd Essex, R.E. Coys, Inf. Bde, Pioneers, and 2nd Ambulances by group system taking one group daily. Animals of these units are all in good condition except from skin disease	/R
"	To.			
"	29th		Two cases of mange previously reigned in 77th Lt. Ambl.; these recovered in three days. Oats forage were examined but nothing found to account for this. Report on these cases sent to A.D.V.S., Reserve Army.	
FLÊTRE	30th		Division moved from BEAUVAL to FLÊTRE by rail	/R
"	31st		Reported arrival therein to M.V.S. to A.D.V.S., Second Army. Inspected billets of M.V.S. Posted T.O. to units. Visited A.D.V.S., 7th Division at BAILLEUL re taking over veterinary arrangements, and inspected billet of his M.V.S.	/R

25th. DIVISION

25th. DIV. A. D. V. S.

NOVEMBER 1916.

Vol 14

Confidential.

War Diary

of

Major W. Ludgate, A.N.C.

A.D.V.S., 25th Division

From Nov. 1st 1916 To Nov. 30th 1916

Volume 14.

Army Form C. 2118.

WAR DIARY
or
INTELLIGENCE SUMMARY.
(Erase heading not required.)

Place	Date	Hour	Summary of Events and Information	Remarks and references to Appendices
FLETRE	November 1916 1		Took over new arrangements from A.D.V.S. 7th Div. Office work, general routine work	W.K.
"	2		Received instructions from D.D.V.S. Second Army re Rabies - examination etc. Sent to dipping baths in process of completion. Roughs for same with D.D.V.S. Second Army.	W.K.
"	3		Arranged for animals transport to the east for remounts re rest to M.V.S. for etc. Re inspection. Rode V.O.s to units of Div. giving instructions re inferences. Visited M.V.S. Inspected billets animals for evacuation.	W.K.
			Held a conference of V.O.s reports returns etc.	
			Moved from FLETRE to BAILLEUL. Inspected billets of M.V.S. at NIEPPE and W.K.	
BAILLEUL	4		general etc. Office general routine work.	W.K.
"	5th 6th 7th		General routine work - visiting units. Transport lines in new area, of boxing N.V.P. to units of the Div. Fetty iremis of the best advantage.	W.K.
			Arranged with 108th F.A. H.Q. for improvements to be made at more this Section re: vaying of stalls, paths, steel troughs, drainage.	W.K.
	8th		Lectured at Animal School on Horse Management Visited mobile Vet. Section to inspect animals for evacuation.	W.K.
	9th		Inspected Horses of 25th Divisional Train - all looking well -	W.K.

WAR DIARY
or
INTELLIGENCE SUMMARY.
(Erase heading not required.)

Army Form C. 2118.

Place	Date	Hour	Summary of Events and Information	Remarks and references to Appendices
BAILLEUL	10th		Arranged with D. Supply Officer for renewal of weekly issue of rum to 148th Bde. It was not given them & must—when regarded as a weather ration—be issued by him. Inspected 4th W. Infy. Bde. transport—Chasseurs. The H.O. Horse lines in unsatisfactory condition & one park being disability sent to D.V.S. - all other animals looking well—sets of wheel chain issued in lieu of drag-ropes shortage of hay ration. Inspected animals of 77th F.F. Ambulance—All looking well & standing except 1 mangy & one. Weekly conference for I.O.— Weekly reports & returns	h.
	11th		Inspected 4th W. Infantry Bde. Transport. All looking well with exception of three number of our horses in Cheshires—they are of horse-type different to the Bath. These had been admitted for treatment recovered. Inspected animals of 745 F. Field Ambulance—All looking well	h.

WAR DIARY
or
INTELLIGENCE SUMMARY.
(Erase heading not required.)

Army Form C. 2118.

(3)

Place	Date	Hour	Summary of Events and Information	Remarks and references to Appendices
BAILLEUL	12.IV.		Inspected 49th Heavy Artillery Group HQ & the Bde— Caddies Room. Brigadier 26 C.R.G.— details & clothes.— Saw a draw for them & the various with regt. of marching orders — Highlands dressed with calcium sulphide powder. Bd. W. Mouat from R.A. Worcester. Those present had recently come out from England. Harris. Hanbell, Gunning Bt. Stn. had already been transported. The first cases had appeared & for past two weeks arranged for a V.P. to inspect all comers & for effective command. Have plenty of reserve.	H.
	13.IV.		Inspected 14th + Bde. R.F.A. 1st Bn 6 Battery. 80th 6 Btn Bde.— 16 Cases of Brigwar. & others. majority very slightly affected — all clipped & dressed with Fr. Lotion— all appear to come with exception of few cases— placed in hospitals— marching orders for a time.	H.

WAR DIARY or INTELLIGENCE SUMMARY

Army Form C. 2118.

Place	Date	Hour	Summary of Events and Information	Remarks and references to Appendices
BAILLEUL	14th		Inspected 105th, 106th & 130th F. Coy. R.E. & 6th D. Mtd. Brdrs. (Pioneers). All troops in good condition — clothing very much better — heavy machines not available from Ordnance — Inspected animals for Scabies by road at Locks W.P. Section	W.
	15th		Inspected 75th F.Y. Bde. Transport. All looking well. Showing soon — arranged for experimental changing of animal in Div. Train of Infantry Transport with Ten Mules. Thoso now to a preserve against picked up mules — light animal in each Bn.D. of front per Coy in Train	W.
	16th		Attended DDVS inspection of Remount Carts at Mobile Vety Section — saw new Remount Standards for the Division	W.
	17th		Handed over duties to Capt. J. Howard Jones RVC. as on my leave	W.
	30th		Leave from Granted from 18th to 29th November. Returned from leave to duty rev from above Officer	W.

25th. DIVISION

25th. DIV. A. D. V. S.

DECEMBER 1916.

Vol 15

Confidential.

War Diary

of

Major W. Redgate, A.V.C.,

A.D.V.S., 25th Division

From Dec. 1st 1916 To Dec. 31st 1916

Volume 15.

WAR DIARY
INTELLIGENCE SUMMARY
(Erase heading not required.)

Army Form C. 2118.

Place	Date Dec 1916	Hour	Summary of Events and Information	Remarks and references to Appendices
BAILLEUL	1–5		Inspector of Hd. Artillery after their return from the SOMME front. Noted all animals in poor condition recommended rest. emaciated and linsed under forwarding numbers in each subsept sector RAC to MVS, Second Army and SVO Division. Also noted areas for immediate evacuation for debility &c. Animals in sick lines were suffering chiefly from cracked heels and necrotic conradenitis the heel and fetlocks.	MR
"	6		Inspected animals at MVS for evacuation – chiefly debility cases. Inspected 49th Heavy Arty Group. Animals in good condition – two areas of improvement moved out of the 40 acres which were remaining in front of this Division.	MR
"	7		Appointed VOs to units of this Division and attached units. Inspected 6th CR Mules Pioneers (Pioneers) – All looking well. Inspected 74th Inf Bde Transport. Two cases at 2nd R.I. Rifles suspected of mange sent to MVS. Issued written instructions to control spread.	MR
"	8		Inspected animals for evacuation at MVS. Office work and reports, and weekly conference for VOs.	MR
"	9		Inspected 113th Bde R.F.A. "D" Batty had 30 cases of ringworm. This batty arrived at HAVRE on 4th Nov. joined the 113th Bde on 30th November on its return from the SOMME.	MR

Army Form C. 2118.

WAR DIARY
or
INTELLIGENCE SUMMARY.
(Erase heading not required.)

Place	Date	Hour	Summary of Events and Information	Remarks and references to Appendices
BAILLEUL	Dec 9th	9/16	Written instructions were issued to all concerned to prevent spread of infection to M.V.S, Boat Army. The designation of this Battery now at ALDERSHOT was 507th Field Batty.	n/a
	10-11		Inspected A.H. Tobe Transport for mange. The following cases which were isolated no suspects were sent to M.V.S. Four from 2nd Royal J. Rifles One from 13th Cheshires One from 11th Lancs Fus. This Infantry transport came from the SOMME by rail on Nov/16 and in my opinion became infected there. Full written instructions to control and stamp out the disease were issued to all concerned. The above cases were all very slightly affected.	n/a
"	12		Inspected 72 Inf Bde Transport. The animals are improving in condition. One case isolated at 151 M.H.G. suspected of mange was sent to M.V.S and preventive measures adopted. No further cases occurred.	n/a
"	13		Inspected 75th Inf Bde. All animals looking well. No mange cases.	n/a
"	14		Inspected 6th Siege Batty attached to this Division just returned from POPERINGHE	n/a

WAR DIARY or INTELLIGENCE SUMMARY

Army Form C. 2118.

(3)

Place	Date	Hour	Summary of Events and Information	Remarks and references to Appendices
BAILLEUL	Dec 14		Up to date stage levelled seven cases of mange in this unit. Sent ten more to M.V.S. six of these were affected and four were slightly mangetouts. Arranged for V.O. to inspect daily, for all inunctions to be at once linked, clipped, singed, and dressed with Calcium Sulphide. Also immediate supply of clipping machine, singing lamp and blow lamp. Drawings and diagrams and full written instructions to all concerned re action taken to M.V.S., 2nd Army. Inspected all surplus animals which were reported as units of this Division after return from SOMME and arranged for their absorption in Division or inspection by D.D.R. re return to Remount Station.	M
"	15		Inspected 49th Div Arty Group. Arranged for re-clipping of ringworm cases. Weekly conference for V.Os. Weekly reports sent in and return.	M
"	16		Inspected 0/112 FABde in which three cases of mange have just been reported. Found no further cases. All preventive measures have been adopted.	M
"	17		Inspected 76th Fd Ambulance transport. Also unit HQ + units. Office work.	M

WAR DIARY

INTELLIGENCE SUMMARY

Army Form C. 2118.

Place	Date Dec 1918	Hour	Summary of Events and Information	Remarks and references to Appendices
BAILLEUL	18-20		Inspected all 174 Artillery Bde with Lt.C. Arthey. Animals in poor condition recommended 2 to be put in armed M.T.S. Rhaed gradually improving. Skinning and sheep satisfactory. Very few animals in sicklines. Chiefly cracked leb and necrotic wounds. There are all improving. Inspected animals for evacuation at M.V.S. Office work. Reports.	MR
"	21		Inspected 25th D.A.C. Condition in No 3 & 4 Sectors good, No 1 & 2 fair. No 2 Section between areas of mange isolated as suspicious, these were sent to M.V.S. — all slightly affected. No 4 Section, one acre mange sent to Vet. Vet. Sec. Preventive measures were recommended to control spread. Inspected animals for evacuation at M.V.S. — Office work and reports.	MR
"	22		Inspected 42 A.T. Co R.E. Three acres under observation for mange. diagnosed Rae. Inspected 195 M.G.Co. Animals in fair condition. Three acres ringworm isolated. Weekly Inference for V.O. Weekly Reports and Returns.	MR
"	23		Inspected animals for evacuation at M.V.S. Chiefly acres from various units of the division and attached units.	MR

WAR DIARY
or
INTELLIGENCE SUMMARY.
(Erase heading not required.)

Army Form C. 2118.

(5)

Place	Date	Hour	Summary of Events and Information	Remarks and references to Appendices
BAILLEUL	DEC 1918 23		Inspected Pioneer (6th S.W.B.) for mange - one case reported. This occurred in a stable on a farm. There were 10 H.D.s in this stable, the other nine were tested no reactors, clipped, singed, shaved, and the stable put in quarantine, full preventive measures used to control. Office work reports. Visited M.V.S. inspected animals for evacuation. -	W.L.
"	24-25		Office work reports. Visited M.V.S. inspected animals for evacuation. - Clifty mange cases.	W.L.
"	26-31		Inspected units of the Division in which mange had occurred, and enquired into measures that were being adopted to control spread.	W.L.

Vol 16

Confidential
War Diary
of
Major W. Ludgate, AVC, ADMS, 25th Div.

from Jan 1st 1917 to Jan 31st 1917

Volume XVI

WAR DIARY
INTELLIGENCE SUMMARY.
(Erase heading not required.)

Army Form C. 2118.

Place	Date	Hour	Summary of Events and Information	Remarks and references to Appendices
BAILEUL	JAN 1/17 1st.		Made daily inspection of units in Division in which many cases occurred, and issued recommendations to control spread.	W.R.
"			Inspected daily cases sent to Mobile X-Ray section for evacuation.	
"	31st.		Office work and general routine work.	

Vol 17

Intelligence Summary
of
Major W. Kerr gate, A.V.C.,
A.D.V.S. 25th Division.

From February 1st to February 28th
1917.

Volume 17.

Original

Army Form C. 2118.

WAR DIARY
INTELLIGENCE SUMMARY.
(Erase heading not required)

Instructions regarding War Diaries and Intelligence Summaries are contained in F.S. Regs., Part II. and the Staff Manual respectively. Title pages will be prepared in manuscript.

Place	Date	Hour	Summary of Events and Information	Remarks and references to Appendices
BAILLEUL	FEB 1917 1st		Made daily inspections of units in the Division for mange. Recommended preventive measures to control spread supervised the carrying out of these measures.	W.L.
			There were 98 slight cases under treatment at unit lines on 1st February. 70 of these were cured during the month. During 28 slight cases under treatment on 28th February.	
	To		21 severe cases of Lymphitis Mange were evacuated during the month. Made inspection of units in which STOMATITIS CONTAGIOSA were reported by executive V.Os. Only one case occurred in each unit viz 110th Bde R.F.A., 112th Bde R.F.A., 125th F.A.C. Visited all units re the disease, re-explained symptoms, preventative measures to be adopted. Issued circular memo re above to all V.Os and units. Inspected abscess cases reported by V.Os sent report to D.V.S., 2nd Army.	W.L.
	28th		Four slight cases of Ulcerative Cellulitis occurred during the month	W.L.

2353 Wt. W2544/F454 700,000 5/15 D.D.&L. A.D.S.S./Forms/C. 2118.

Army Form C. 2118.

WAR DIARY
INTELLIGENCE SUMMARY.
(Erase heading not required.)

Instructions regarding War Diaries and Intelligence Summaries are contained in F. S. Regs., Part II. and the Staff Manual respectively. Title pages will be prepared in manuscript.

Place	Date	Hour	Summary of Events and Information	Remarks and references to Appendices
BAILLEUL	FEB 1917		Three men sent to Mob. Vt. Sectn for treatment. Infected animals at Mob. Vt. Sectn sent for evacuation and treatment daily.	W.L.

Vol 18

Confidential

Intelligence Summary

by

Major W. Lutgate, D.V.C.

A.D.V.S., 25th Division

From March 1st 1917 to March 31st 1917.

Volume XVIII

Army Form C. 2118.

WAR DIARY
or
INTELLIGENCE SUMMARY.
(Erase heading not required.)

Place	Date	Hour	Summary of Events and Information	Remarks and references to Appendices
	MARCH 1917 1st to 31st.		Daily inspection of units of this Division for range etc noting numbers of animals in poor condition for special feeding — linseed cake and crushed oats. All cases of mange that were under treatment at unit lines & M.V.S. have been cured. No fresh cases have recurred. A few cases of STOMATITIS CONTAGIOSA occurred in units during the month, but were diagnosed early and no further cases appeared. Animals of field ambulances and red xxx fell off in condition when put on 3/4 ration of oats, especially when hay left stables at NIEPPE area, marched to IIIrd Army training area on 26-2-17. These picketted in the open. These animals have all been noted. Those in the Divisional Artillery have been recommended for full scale of oats. All these animals	M.R.

Place	Date	Hour	Summary of Events and Information	Remarks and references to Appendices
	MARCH 1st to 31st (cont)		Are now getting linseed cake from 1 - 1½ lbs daily in an extra fruit from the allowance of 10 centimes per animal per day. (Authority D.D.S.T. 2nd Army S/801/16 dated 23-3-1917.) This allows for 18.00 lbs of linseed cake for this Division daily. Mule daily inspection of animals under treatment for evacuation at Mob. Vet. Section. Recently Horse Line Duty Men visiting cases from Artillery Regs and D.A.C. Arrange for skinning of animals that die or are destroyed at waggon transport lines, and for hides to be sent to Mob. Vet. Section for disposal.	

D.A.G.
  Base.
———

Herewith War Diary of A.D.V.S.
25th Division for April 1917.

12/5/17.

[signature]
for Major General
Commanding 25th Divn.

Confidential. '25
Vol 19

Intelligence Summary
of
Major W. Lagate, A.V.C.,
A.D.V.S., 25th Division.

From April 1st To April 30th
1917.

Volume XIX

WAR DIARY / INTELLIGENCE SUMMARY

Army Form C. 2118.

Place	Date	Hour	Summary of Events and Information	Remarks and references to Appendices
BAILLEUL	April		Made daily inspection of animals of Division with V.Os i/c units noting one to be sent to M.V.S. for evacuation also animals in poor condition for special feeding (eg cooked oats, steamed oats, boiled linseed, linseed cake etc) at unit lines. For light duty. Those animals were examined for and of poor condition, if received their teeth were rasped, they were attended to for worms. Several cases of mange recurred in areas that had been under treatment the Winter. These were sent for further treatment to M.V.S. on it severe evacuated. Animals of this Division were kept in full scale of ration from April 21st since that time their condition has improved greatly of M.V.S. on steaming raring of fodder. & N.Cos men from neighbouring units. A class of instruction was given to Instructors who gave fitting & adjusting harness, saddlery was also given attention. Daily routine of office work. Weekly Returns Reports & Conferences for V.O.	

Vol 20

Confidential

War Diary

of

Major W. Lingate A.V.C.

ADVS, 25th Division

From May 1st 1917 To May 31st 1917.

Volume XX

WAR DIARY
INTELLIGENCE SUMMARY.
(Erase heading not required.)

Army Form C. 2118.

Place	Date	Hour	Summary of Events and Information	Remarks and references to Appendices
RAVELSBERG	1917		The daily inspection of animals of the Division with V.O. i/c units noting cases to be sent to the M.V. Section for evacuation. These were chiefly debility cases in animals of defective conformation that failed to condition in tin lines.	
			All animals in poor condition are noted and recommendation for careful sets for these animals for a period of three weeks forwarded to O.C.'s, Leend Army and sanctioned.	
			Animals the required re-branding with broad arrow were noted and sent to M.V.S. for this purpose.	
			Inspected shoeing of all units in this Division sent reports to "Q" on units in which shoeing was defective or behind-hand, noting units in which shoeing tools required replacing, also in which farriery establishment was deficient.	
			Several cases of mange received during the month and were sent to M.V.S. for evacuation, if severe, and for treatment return to units if slight. Written directions to control spread were forwarded to units concerned and to veterinary officers.	

WAR DIARY
INTELLIGENCE SUMMARY.
(Erase heading not required.)

Army Form C. 2118.

Instructions regarding War Diaries and Intelligence Summaries are contained in F. S. Regs., Part II. and the Staff Manual respectively. Title pages will be prepared in manuscript.

Place	Date	Hour	Summary of Events and Information	Remarks and references to Appendices
RAVELSBERG 28.S.17.Central	(Continued)		Inspected surplus fresh animals in the Division for return to Remount Section.	W.h.
			Reports were forwarded to ADVS, 2nd Army re 25 Division Q.M. Advisability of issuing a mule also No 15½ size.	W.h.
			1. Complaints regarding present pattern of nosebags suffered of nose reed.	
	May 1917		As to ADVS, 2nd Army on suitability to stand hardship of campaigning of the various breeds of animals represented in the Army in France	W.h.
			Daily routine of office work	
			Weekly conference for veterinary officers	
			Weekly Reports and Returns	

Confidential.

War Diary

of

Major W. Lingard, A.V.C.,

A.D.V.S., 25th Division

From June 1st 1917 To June 30th 1917

Volume XXI

WAR DIARY
INTELLIGENCE SUMMARY.
(Erase heading not required.)

Army Form C. 2118.

Place	Date	Hour	Summary of Events and Information	Remarks and references to Appendices
RAYELSBURG CAMP N.Z. Central	1917		Inspection of units attached to the Division for administration viz:-	
	JUNE 1st to 21st		24th A.F.A. Bde with V.O i/c Capt J.E.YOUNG A.V.C. Condition of artillery horses good. Supply sector (H.D.) Horses attached strength 22. Were dirty and ungroomed. One case of mange sent to M.V.S. for evacuation. Report on condition of these animals sent to D.D.C. Bde, D.S.R. N.Z. "D".	WK
			03rd A.F.A. Bde "V.O i/c sent G.FRAYNE A.V.C. Condition of artillery animals fair. Supply Sector Hos dirty ungroomed. Ungroomed. 8 cases of mange from this unit, and Polished 23 cases slightly affected under treatment at unit lines. Report sent to DCRBde, DSR N.Z "D", and MVS, Second Army.	WK
			2d N.Z.A.F.A. Bde. V.O i/c Capt A.TAYLOR, N.Z.V.C. Condition good. Mange Nil.	WK
			242 A.F.A. Bde V.O i/c Capt C.G.HEARNE, A.V.C. Condition good. Two cases of mange in R.A.C. evacuated.	WK
			Inspected reinforcements to Willis Rest of 19 horses and 37 mules (Remounts) which joined 03rd A.F.A. Bde. Horses sent to M.V.S., Second Army.	WK
			Daily inspection of units of this Division and of animals for evacuation and treatment at M.V.S.	

WAR DIARY or INTELLIGENCE SUMMARY.

Army Form C. 2118.

Place	Date	Hour	Summary of Events and Information	Remarks and references to Appendices
RAVELSBURG CAMP 3 A.S.D. Vet.	1917		Army veterinary operations in the taking of MESSINES RIDGE (June 5th to 21st) 30	
			sick animals were evacuated chiefly by Barge to Receiving Veterinary Hospital	
			ST OMER from this Division and 21 animals were killed by shell fire. The	
			casualties occurred amongst about 1000 animals working in the intense shell	
			area, chiefly when bringing up ammunition and returns in the rails	
			attached for administration. 10 were killed and 5 evacuated.	
			The animals of this Division maintained and kept their condition	
			although the weather was very hot and the moth trying. This was owing to good	
			watering arrangements, good grazing which were taken full advantage of,	
			and by careful supervision they kept free from contagious disease, which	
			was liable to spread owing to concentration and mixing up of units	
			in the Divisional Area.	
	June 22nd		Handed over to A.D.V.S., 3rd Australian Division prior to this	
			Division moving into rest area giving map position of units and means of	

Army Form C. 2118.

WAR DIARY
or
INTELLIGENCE SUMMARY.
(Erase heading not required.)

(3)

Place	Date 1917	Hour	Summary of Events and Information	Remarks and references to Appendices
RAVELSBURG CAMP	Sept 22nd		Veterinary Officers in charge of units remaining in the area.	
	" 23rd		Office moved with D.H.Q. from RAVELSBURG Camp to BAILLEUL. M.V.S. marched from RAVELSBURG to ST HILAIRE	
BAILLEUL				
BOMY	" 24th		This office with D.H.Q. moved from BAILLEUL to BOMY. M.V.S. marched from ST HILAIRE to LUGY. Inspected billets of M.V.S. at LUGY.	
"	" 25th		Appointed V.Os to units in rest area, giving each positions of transport lines.	
"	26th		Inspections of units in rest area. Only two animals were left behind	
"	30th		on line of march. These were reported to M.V.S. for collection.	

Confidential

Vol 22

Intelligence Summary

of

Major W. Lndgate, A.V.C.

D.A.D.V.S., 25th Division.

From July 1st 1917 to July 31st 1917.

Volume XXII.

WAR DIARY
INTELLIGENCE SUMMARY.
(Erase heading not required.)

Army Form C. 2118.

Place	Date	Hour	Summary of Events and Information	Remarks and references to Appendices
BOMY	JULY 1st		Proceeded on leave to Ireland. Capt J.H. Jones AVC acted for me when H	AK
			leave	
BUSSEBOOM	12th		Returned from leave and took over from Capt J.H. Jones AVC	AK
			The following units have been attached to this Division for administration	
			33rd Bde R.F.A	
			41st Bde R.F.A	
			2nd Bn C.R.E	
			15th 2a C.R.E	
			9th H. 2a C.R.E	
			2nd D.L.I (Pioneers)	
			6th M.G.C	
			6th Div Signal Coy	
			HQ Coy Ch Sch Depot	
			HQ Gen Dir RA+RE	9.H. Anivorix
			2nd Army Troops Coy R.E	

WAR DIARY
INTELLIGENCE SUMMARY.
(Erase heading not required.)

Army Form C. 2118.

Place	Date	Hour	Summary of Events and Information	Remarks and references to Appendices
BUSSEBOOM	JULY (D.R.(Cont)		232 Army St Coy RFA	
			277 " " "	
			67 " " "	
			38 " " "	
			Inspected all animals at MVS for operation	
	13th		with suspicious cases on sputum from No 1 Sectn S.K. MG. Squadron	
			negative	
	14th		Reported above cases to ADVS IInd Corps, and inspected the animal	
			Reactor to second intradermal test also negative. Animal was put north	
			for re-testing in three weeks time.	
			One case of skin spots (Monomlcer) admitted today from 57th Batty	
			45th Bde RFA. 5th Dragoon are fund on arrival at MVS to be affected	
			with skin itch contagion. This animal was immediately segregated	
			and reported to ADVS IInd Corps, and M.O. 7th Dragoons to be informed	
			(animals (40 up Bde) are on line at L6 Lime the animal was sent in)	
			Trade out list giving number of animals there require dipping	

WAR DIARY
INTELLIGENCE SUMMARY

Army Form C. 2118.

Place	Date	Hour	Summary of Events and Information	Remarks and references to Appendices
	JULY			
BUSSEBOOM	14th (cont)		for units of this Division and attached units and forwarded it to ADMS II Corps	
			Corps. Attended conference at office of ADMS II Corps	
			Inspected all animals at MVS for evacuation. Chiefly old wounds.	
"	15th		Inspected 23rd A.F.A. Bde with V.O. in charge. Sent three cases of mange to MVS for evacuation. Office work and reports.	
"	16th to 18th		Inspector of 25th Div Artillery. Sent 6 cases of mange to MVS for evacuation. Sent 110 R.Bde R.F.A. animals are from 25th Div. Daily inspection of animals at MVS for evacuation and treatment. Office work and reports.	
"	19th		Visited one suitable position for an Advanced Vety Aid Bn. also received words from Aid Post & MVS recommended by O.MVS and the N.C.O. to be placed in charge of the Post. Sent out positions to ADVS, Third Corps and 25th Division R	
"	20th		Usual instruction on fitting and dusting gas blankets on transport animals of this Division. Weekly conference of this Division. Inspectors of various units of this Division, attacked units with V.Os in charge	

WAR DIARY
INTELLIGENCE SUMMARY
(Erase heading not required.)

Army Form C. 2118.

Place	Date	Hour	Summary of Events and Information	Remarks and references to Appendices
BUSSEBOOM	JULY 21st		Attended conference at office of A.D.V.S. Ind Corps. Inspected all sick area of mange under treatment at unit lines of 25th Divisional A.F.A. Bdes attached to this Division.	A/L
"	22nd		Attended inspection of 37 M.V.S. by A.D.V.S. Fifth Army. Inspected all animals at M.V.S. for evacuation. Office work.	A/L
"	23rd		Established a Divisional Segregation Camp for the treatment of all slightly affected mange cases from units of this Division.	A/L
"	24th		Daily inspection of units of this Division and attached units; also of animals under treatment at Div. Segregation Camp and animals for evacuation.	A/L
"	31st		At M.V.S. Office work and general routine work.	

Vol 23

Confidential

Intelligence Summary

of

Major W. Lutgate, A.V.C.

D.A.D.V.S., 25th Division

From August 1st 1917 To August 31st 1917.

Volume XXIII.

WAR DIARY
INTELLIGENCE SUMMARY
(Erase heading not required.)

Army Form C. 2118.

Place	Date	Hour	Summary of Events and Information	Remarks and references to Appendices
BUSSEBOOM	AUG 1917 1st		Inspected 110 Bde R.F.A for strangles reference case from Horse Veterinary Hospital Plt. One case had been sent from the 37 Mob Vet Section belonging to this Brigade. Found	
"	To		Brigade free from strangles. Case referred to was a case of Stomatitis. Surface scrape taken by the animals showing a Clinical Hylsick Bull, but this information	
"	3rd		was omitted from the Evacuation Roll sent by the Mob Vet Section	
"	4th		Daily inspection of units of this Division. Cases of slight mange were sent to Divisional Segregation Camp for treatment and return to unit when cured.	
STEENVOORDE	To		Inspection of animals for evacuation at Mob Vet Section and animals under treatment at Div Segregation Camp.	
	(FROM 17th inst)		Weekly Conferences for V.Os of the Division. Office and general routine work.	
	31st			
			August 17th. Division in rest.	
			Capt E. BIRKIN, A.V.C (T.C) was evacuated sick as a result of an accident an	
			Aug 17th. Capt J HILL A.V.C V.O if 38 Bde R.F.A. Bde was sent in very charge	
			temporarily of 110 Bde R.F.A until relief arrived. Capt W. HAMILTON, A.V.C.	

Army Form C. 2118.

WAR DIARY
or
INTELLIGENCE SUMMARY.
(Erase heading not required.)

Place	Date	Hour	Summary of Events and Information	Remarks and references to Appendices
	Aug 1917		(T.C.) reported for duty with 110th A. Bde R.F.A. from No 4 Veterinary Hospital, CALAIS on 25-8-17.	

Vol 24

Confidential

Intelligence Summary

of

Major W. Redgate, F.V.C.

D.A.D.V.S., 25th Division

From Sept 1st/917 To Sept 30/12/917

Volume XXIV.

Army Form C. 2118.

WAR DIARY
INTELLIGENCE SUMMARY.
(Erase heading not required.)

Instructions regarding War Diaries and Intelligence Summaries are contained in F. S. Regs., Part II. and the Staff Manual respectively. Title pages will be prepared in manuscript.

Place	Date	Hour	Summary of Events and Information	Remarks and references to Appendices
	Sept 1917			
STEENVOORDE	1		Inspection of animals for evacuation at MVS. Animals under treatment 651. Egyptian Camp for mange. Inspection of 6th Hussars and Ambulance. Animals generally good, grooming good, shoeing satisfactory.	HR
	2		Officers and 37 M.V.S. moved with Hqrs Division from STEENVOORDE to RENINGHELST.	HR
RENINGHELST			Inspected kits of MVS at RENINGHELST	
	3		Posting of VOs to units in new area. Inspection of 37 animals at MVS for evacuation landed over by M.V.S. of 23rd Division marching out. 27 also had to be destroyed for incurable injuries.	
	4 & 5		Inspection of 112R 15th RFA and 25th DAC. Condition, grooming & shoeing good. To mange. Two cases of ringworm in No 2 section 25th DAC sent to Divl Segregation Camp for treatment.	HR
	6		Inspection of equipment at M.V.S. Animals for evacuation treatment. Inspected 25th Div Train. All animals in good condition. Grooming & shoeing good.	HR

A6945 Wt. W14426/M1160 350,000 12/16 D. D. & L. Forms/C./2118/14.

WAR DIARY
INTELLIGENCE SUMMARY

Army Form C. 2118.

Place	Date Sept 1917	Hour	Summary of Events and Information	Remarks and references to Appendices
	6	(cont)	Weekly Conference for V.Os. Weekly reports and returns.	AR
	7		Inspection of 10th Bde R.F.A. Two left wing are in "A"Batty. One in "A"Batty sent to Segregation Camp for treatment. Condition of "A","B" and "C" Batteries fair. "D" Batty good. Grooming and shoeing satisfactory.	AR
	8		Attended Conference at office of ADVS I Anzac Corps	AR
	9		Inspected 75 road and 12 train cases at MVS for evacuation. Inspection of RE Coy and Pioneers. Condition grooming and shoeing satisfactory. Office and MVS moved from SCOTTISH CAMP, RENINGHELST to LABEUVRIERE.	AR
LABEUVRIERE	10		AUCHEL area with Anzac Division. Inspected billets of MVS at FONTENELLE FARM. Posted VOs to units in new area.	AR
	11		Visited ADVS I Corps. Arranged for evacuation by barge and train from BETHUNE. Office work etc.	AR
	12 to 16		Inspection of Inf Bde Groups with AA and QMG, 25th Division	AR

WAR DIARY
INTELLIGENCE SUMMARY
(Erase heading not required.)

Army Form C. 2118.

Place	Date	Hour	Summary of Events and Information	Remarks and references to Appendices
	Sept 1917 17/18/19		Inspection of all units of this Division with ADVS, I Corps.	APR
	20 to 26		Daily inspection of units of this Division, animals at MVS for evacuation and treatment, also animals at Sub Coys & units. Arrangements for mange in inquorum.	APR
	27		Attended Committee composed of D.D.Remounts, Vet Army, ADVS, I Corps, Horse Master I Corps, re inspection of mares with a view to finding any suitable for breeding purposes. Units inspected 25th Div Artillery and 196 Coy ASC.	APR
	28		14 cases of influenza (mild form of Pink Eye) occurred in 199 Coy ASC. Inspected the Coy and arranged for a field to segregate these cases. Issued necessary instructions to control spread.	APR
	29		Inspected 75th Fd Ambulance, 74th Inf Bde HdQrs, 13th Cheshires, 11th Lines, Trailors, Ordnance, watering posts. Shoeing satisfactory. Office work, weekly reports sent in return.	

WAR DIARY
INTELLIGENCE SUMMARY.
(Erase heading not required.)

Army Form C. 2118.

Place	Date	Hour	Summary of Events and Information	Remarks and references to Appendices
	Sept 1917			
	29		Attended conference of A.D.V.S., I Corps at his office. Inspection of animals at M.V.S. for evacuation and those at Civil Segregation Camp under treatment. Office work.	
	30		Inspected 7th Inf. Bde Transport. Condition and grooming good; shoeing satisfactory	

Confidential.

Intelligence Summary

of

Major W. Lidgate, A.V.C.,

D.A.D.V.S., 25th Division.

From October 1st 1917 To October 31st 1917.

Volume XXV.

WAR DIARY
INTELLIGENCE SUMMARY

Army Form C. 2118.

Place	Date	Hour	Summary of Events and Information	Remarks and references to Appendices
LABEUVRIERE	October 1st 1917		Inspection of animals for evacuation at M.V.S. and animals under treatment at Sick Segregation Bunks. Office and general routine work.	
"	2nd		Inspected 25th Div Train. Condition, grooming and shoeing good. Sent animals of 200thB/ASC to Vet conditioning; two of them sent to M.V.S. for evacuation.	
"	3rd		Inspector of Transfers from 25th Div Artillery to 46th Div Artillery in reduction of establishment of D.A.C. Eight of them sent to MVS for evacuation on account of poor condition etc. Office and general routine work at MVS and Sick Segregation Camp.	
"	4th		Inspected 105th M.G. Coy. Condition rubbing good, grooming unsatisfactory. Sent two mules to Sick Segregation Camp. Body examination of range for clipping and further examination. Prov Capt. J.FORREST, A.V.C. O.C. 37 MVS in temporary charge of 7th & 74th Sqs Bde Groups during absence of Capt. J. HOWARD JONES A.V.C. on leave, and took over charge of No 37 M.V.S. Nine Bde Groups march from rest area to forward area Bolay. Inspected Bde Groups on line of march. Returned two cases of ringworm to	

A6945 Wt. W14422/M1160 350,000 12/16 D. D. & L. Forms/C./2118/14.

WAR DIARY or INTELLIGENCE SUMMARY

Army Form C. 2118.

Place	Date October 1917	Hour	Summary of Events and Information	Remarks and references to Appendices
LABEUVRIERE	4th (cont)		74th Bde from Legerplain Camp arrd.	
	5th		Weekly reports and returns. Started over billet of MVS to OBLINGHEM, 2nd Division. Attended inspection of A.D.Remnts. First dump of animals prepared for casting.	WR
	6th		Reported standing to "D" occupied by mange cases is new area. These not to be reoccupied—disinfected and fenced by me. Inspected billets for MVS at ESSARS. Did not like new billet occupied by MVS, 2nd Division, in BETHUNE as too far away from A.D.Dn. and not in our area.	WR / WR
LOCON	7th		Office moved with D.H.Q. to LOCON. Marched with MVS to new billet at ESSARS.	WR
"	8th		Inspection of MVS and Legerplain Camp. Inspected 74th Bde transport. Condition good; grooming & rubbing satisfactory. Hattes improved since last inspection when many of the mules' feet were too long. Sent one H.D. from 11th Lanc. Fusiliers to MVS for evacuation, affected with mange. Inspected 130th Bd Ay R.E. Condition etc good. Due animals sent 6	WR

WAR DIARY
INTELLIGENCE SUMMARY.
(Erase heading not required.)

Army Form C. 2118.

Instructions regarding War Diaries and Intelligence Summaries are contained in F. S. Regs., Part II. and the Staff Manual respectively. Title pages will be prepared in manuscript.

Place	Date October 1917	Hour	Summary of Events and Information	Remarks and references to Appendices
LOOON	8th (Sun)		M.V.S. Pt. evacuation, Clinic Laneries, Stores and Jighbones. Routine work at M.V.S. and Segregation Camp.	N/R
"	9th		Inspected 7th Inf. Bde Transport. Conditions etc good. Ent. Staff Captain's cheque to Div Segregation Camp suspicious of Epizootic Lymphangitis. Symptoms. Several small abscesses one place on cheek following in hit injury. Smears examined at M.V.S. negative. Sample of fluid also sent to A.V.C. Bacteriological Laboratory B.E.F. Result negative for Epizootic Lymphangitis only pyogenic organisms found. Abscesses etc. toned up, and the animal was discharged to duty. Sent me case of mange from 7th M.G. Coy to M.V.S. for evacuation. This was a transfer from 2nd D.A.C. received two days ago. Reported this to A.D.V.S., XI Corps and N.A.N.S., 2nd Division.	N/R
"	10th Oct		Inspected 7th and 75th Inf Bde Trains with A.D.V.S., XI Corps. Conditions	N/R
"	11th		grooming shoeing etc good. Improvements necessary to transport lines were noted & reported to 2 I/c Div "Q".	N/R
"	12th		Weekly conference for V.Os when Epizootic Lymphangitis and Mange	N/R

Army Form C. 2118.

WAR DIARY
or
INTELLIGENCE SUMMARY.
(Erase heading not required.)

Instructions regarding War Diaries and Intelligence Summaries are contained in F. S. Regs., Part II. and the Staff Manual respectively. Title pages will be prepared in manuscript.

Place	Date October 1917	Hour	Summary of Events and Information	Remarks and references to Appendices
LOCON	12th (cont)		Athletics were discussed, reference preventive measures, dressing of wounds etc. Visited some 6 all units through "D" re improvements on stable management, wire hay nets, racks, sieves, picking tiles etc etc.	
"	13th		Inspection of NVS animals under treatment at Dis: Segregation Amb. Inspected No 1 Sqn 7SC, condition etc very good. Inspected 25th DAC, condition etc good — 2 cases of ringworm in No 2 Section under treatment.	
"	14th		One case of Stomatitis Contagiosa discovered in 12th Cheshires. Transfer one week ago from Rd MVS. Reported this to ADVS XI Corps and DDVS, 2nd Division. This animal showed no symptoms on arrival at unit, but was isolated in the usual way. No further case occurred.	
"	15th		Inspected all very mullets M/Gs sheds in charge with T.O. and A.V.C. Sergeants concerned; made note of instruments deficient or unserviceable. Intents made out to replace.	
"	16th		Visited 1st Bde, saw CRSO re clipping of animals under instruction from COO division.	

Army Form C. 2118.

WAR DIARY
INTELLIGENCE SUMMARY.
(Erase heading not required.)

Instructions regarding War Diaries and Intelligence Summaries are contained in F. S. Regs., Part II. and the Staff Manual respectively. Title pages will be prepared in manuscript.

Place	Date	Hour	Summary of Events and Information	Remarks and references to Appendices
LOCON	October 1917 17th		Visited B/110th Bde RFA re cases of sand colic due to animals eating litter. Sent instructions re preventive measures to be adopted through 25th Div. "Q".	
			Attended inspection of detachments First Army of animals prepared for casting.	
			Inspected 74th Inf Bde Coops with PDVS, XI Corps. Condition etc good. Two cases of Ophthalmia in 74th M.G. Coy. Their rules of infirmaries required to supply standards reported to 25th Div "Q".	
	18th		Visited M.V.S. and Div Segregation Camp. Office work.	
	19th		Inspected 110th Bde RFA with V.O. in charge; also 2n/3 Section D.A.C. Condition not good. "D Batty 17n/3 Section DAC condition etc very good. Sent to A. B. and C. Batteries 110th Bde very much improved in past month. Two cases of Ophthalmia more placentae cellulitis to M.V.S. from 110th & 112th RFA. To cure of mange in above units.	
	20th		Weekly conference for V.Os.; weekly reports return. Office work and general routine work.	

WAR DIARY
INTELLIGENCE SUMMARY

Army Form C. 2118.

(Erase heading not required.)

Instructions regarding War Diaries and Intelligence Summaries are contained in F.S. Regs., Part II. and the Staff Manual respectively. Title pages will be prepared in manuscript.

Place	Date	Hour	Summary of Events and Information	Remarks and references to Appendices
LOCON.	October 1917 21st		Inspected 112th Bde R.F.A. with V.O. in charge. Condition etc very good.	
			Mayor N.L. Saw class of decorative abilities for Officers to M.V.S. for evacuation.	
			Attended conference at office of ADMS, XI Corps.	
"	22nd		Inspected animals for evacuation at M.V.S.	
			Inspected 106th & 3rd Coy R.E. re no case of suspicious mange reported.	
			Sent in further orders.	
"	23rd		Inspected 41st TMB units, 25th Signal Coy, 95th M.G. Coy also 6th & S. Wales Borderers (Pioneers). Condition of above units good. Approaches to lines of Pioneers 7/95 M.G. Coy bad. Reported to "Q". The range to Gorkhulvin in above units.	
"	24th		Inspected reactions to mallein of 4th N. South Staffords which nearly joined this Division from England. All reactions negative.	
			Inspected 77th & 91st Ambulance. Condition etc good. Orders of veterinary outfit visit clear really kept. Reported this to O.C. and V.O. in charge. Sent required for above.	
"	25th		Visited Advanced Remount Section to close charges for A.O.C.	

A6945 Wt. W11422/M1160 350,000 12/16 D.D.& L. Forms/C./2118/14.

WAR DIARY
INTELLIGENCE SUMMARY.
(Erase heading not required.)

Army Form C. 2118.

Place	Date	Hour	Summary of Events and Information	Remarks and references to Appendices
LOCON	October 25th 1917 (cont)		Division and D.A.A.G. Inspected animals for evacuation & treatment at M.V.S. and Sick Segregation Camp.	W.D
"	26th		Inspected M.V.S, 7th Inf Bde Transport and 130th Bty of R.F.A with A.T.V.S.". 21st Army Division shoeing also very good. Shoeing of S.R.L. Nizams require re flooring. Reported this to 25th Divn "Q".	W.D
"	27th		Inspected 110th Bde R.F.A with V.O in charge, reference one case of mange and one case of Lice reported in "A" Battery. To further cases detected. Issued precautions to control. Sent affected animals to M.V.S.	W.D
"	28th		Inspected animals for evacuation & treatment at M.V.S and Sick Segregation Camp. Inspected 77th Fd Ambulance, refering equipment now clean and well kept. Sent me one of lymph-glands to M.V.S. for evacuation. Inspected 4th South Staffords Transport. Condition good. Shoeing	W.D
"	29th		much behind hand. To sleep yet received. Shoeing done by 200th Coy 172C. Saw N.A.V.O.S re shoes and asked to listen to shipping time yet. Asked for timeline to be sent from H.Q., 7th Inf Bde.	W.D

Army Form C. 2118.

WAR DIARY
INTELLIGENCE SUMMARY.
(Erase heading not required.)

Instructions regarding War Diaries and Intelligence Summaries are contained in F. S. Regs., Part II. and the Staff Manual respectively. Title pages will be prepared in manuscript.

Place	Date	Hour	Summary of Events and Information	Remarks and references to Appendices
LOCON	October 1917 29th (Cont)		Visited M.V.S. and arranged for treatment of one mange case for 110th Bde R.F.A. at sulphur chamber (experimental). Inspected animals for evacuation.	
"	30th		Inspected 25th Div. Train. One suspected mange case from Post Coy sent to Divl. Segregation Camp for examination.	
"	31st		Inspected 110 Hr Bde R.F.A. reference one case of mange that occurred. Found another case indeed suspicious of mange. Sent to Divl. Segregation Camp for further examination. Scrapings taken and examined; result negative.	

Vol 26.

Confidential

Intelligence Summary

of

M.A.D.V.S. 25th Division.

From Nov 1st 1917 To Nov 30th 1917.

Volume XXVI.

WAR DIARY / INTELLIGENCE SUMMARY.

(Erase heading not required.)

Army Form C. 2118.

Instructions regarding War Diaries and Intelligence Summaries are contained in F. S. Regs., Part. II. and the Staff Manual respectively. Title pages will be prepared in manuscript.

Place	Date	Hour	Summary of Events and Information	Remarks and references to Appendices
LOCON	Jan 1917 1st		Inspection of animals under treatment and those under observation for mange at 61st Segregation Camp; also animals for evacuation at MVS. Inspected remounts for this Division on arrival.	J.R.
"	2nd		Weekly conference for V/Os. Weekly reports and returns. Inspected 110th Bde RFA with ADVS, XI Corps. Condition, grooming and shoeing good. Very few animals on sick lines. Mange Nil. Veterinary equipment complete and well kept.	J.R.
"	3rd		Inspected 76th Fd. Ambulance. Condition etc good. Sick Nil. Office and general routine work. Visited MVS and Segregation Camp. Attended conference of ADsVS, XI Corps.	J.R.
"	4th		Inspected 112th Bde RFA. Condition grooming and shoeing very good. Very few animals on sick lines. Mange Nil. Veterinary equipment complete and well looked after.	J.R.
"	5th		Inspection of animals at MVS Segregation Camp. Inspected 198 Coy ASC. Condition grooming etc very good. Two slight injuries on sick lines. Office work reports.	J.R.

WAR DIARY

INTELLIGENCE SUMMARY.

(Erase heading not required.)

Army Form C. 2118.

Place	Date Nov 1917	Hour	Summary of Events and Information	Remarks and references to Appendices
LOCON	6th		Inspected 136 th 2d Coy R.E. for Scabies. Strathie Contagion reference one case reported in a remount which was sent on November 1st. Affected one sent to 33rd Mobile Separation Camp, and reported by wire to A.D.V.S., XI Corps and to V.Os of this Division. Infected all remounts which arrived in this British. Issued necessary precautions to control spread. No further cases occurred.	1/2
"	7th		Visited all 2nd Line Section MG of 25th Div Artillery, examined Officers & N.Cos and issued reference reporting all minor Sneezes slight to A/C sergeants for keeping unstruth A/C sergeants on method of nursing the adopted as a precaution against Epizootic Lymphangitis.	1/2
"	8th		Handed over duties to Capt J. FORREST, A/C and proceeded on leave to England.	1/2

WAR DIARY
INTELLIGENCE SUMMARY.

Army Form C. 2118.

(Erase heading not required.)

Place	Date Nov 1917	Hour	Summary of Events and Information	Remarks and references to Appendices
LOCON	8th		Office routine work. Inspected animals for evacuation at M.V.S. Carried out Stock Segregation Camp. Inspected 201 Coy. T.C., 77th 3rd Auk. & 25th Signal Coy. Condition grooming being good. Reported to A.D.V.S., XI Corps re case of strangles.	/F
"	9th		Inspected D.H.Q. & J.H.Q. R.E. Executive work.	/F
"	10th		Saw "Q" re distribution of steel plates as preventive from P.U.N. Visited Horse Butchers in BETHUNE with interpreter re Empira received for animals. Arranged for projectile buyer to see animal before removing force. Inspection 75th Field T.H.Q. stranded mare of E.V.C. in Brood war.	/F
"	11th		Inspected animals for evacuation at M.V.S. Attended inspection of Brood mares by War Office committee	/F
"	12th		Inspected 194 Coy A.S.C. Condition, grooming & being good. Examined suspicious case of strangles.	/F
"	13th		Inspected by A.D.V.S, XI Corps. as Visiting Officer.	/F
"	14th		Inspected 112 R.F.A. & R.F.A. with A.D.V.S, XI Corps. The equipment and kept Condition grooming & being good.	/F
"	15		Routine work at M.V.S. Executive duties.	/F

WAR DIARY
INTELLIGENCE SUMMARY.
(Erase heading not required.)

Army Form C. 2118.

Place	Date Nov 1917	Hour	Summary of Events and Information	Remarks and references to Appendices
LOCON	16th		Conference of VOs. Visited APO & inspected care of runf, spent it 6. Segregation Camp.	I.T.
"	17th		Inspected remounts at 196 Coy ACC. Battle sheep of animal.	I.T.
"	18th		Report re Ophthalmia sent to ADVS XI Corps	I.T.
"	19th		Invalided mule of 77th Sd Amb for glanders. Inspected animals for erysipelas	I.T.
"	20th		at M.V.S. Those in Segregation Camp. Inspected 196 Coy ACC for mange. Examined civilian horse in BETHUNE reported had case of mange. Tested it at Segregation Camp & finally handed it over to M.V.S. 42 addsr. on having appeared on Nov 29th.	I.T.
"	21st		Executive work.	I.T.
"	22nd		Conference for VOs. Inspected animals for evacuation at M.V.S.	I.T.
"	23rd		Executive work.	I.T.
"	24th		Inspected part of 166 Hy Batty RGA for ringworm - 16 cases ringworm & 1 of Ophthalmia.	I.T.
"	25th		Inspected remainder of 16A Hy Batty at BETHUNE - 7 cases of mange. ADVS arranged for segregation of mange ringworm in BETHUNE lines.	I.T.

WAR DIARY

INTELLIGENCE SUMMARY.

(Erase heading not required.)

Army Form C. 2118.

Place	Date	Hour	Summary of Events and Information	Remarks and references to Appendices
LOCON	Nov 1917 26th		Took over duties of M.V.N.S. from Major Ralph, V.O. who returned from leave today.	/T.
"	27th		Arranged for billet for M.V.S. at BOMY. Arr. of Marston & Nott'll reported to 2nd Corps D.A.D. Animal tested with mullein 9pm same day.	/T.
"	28th		Reported formally to D.A.V.S. XI Corps informed above arr. Perston. Inner eyelid fairly large of mullein reac. painful. D.S.V.S examined negative reac. Instructed V.O. that with neck mullein in afternoon. & positive result the inner negative result.	/T.
GREUPPE	29th		D.H.Q. moved to GREUPPE in First Army Area. Reported location of M.V.S. office M.V.S. & D.D.V.S. I Corps.	/T.
	30th		Investigator reported at 20.1 Coy M.T.A at LE HAMEL. Very good class of transport. Inspected 136th Bty R.E. more care of harness.	/T.

Vol 27

— Confidential —

War Diary

of

Major G.D. Norman, A.V.C.,

D.A.D.V.S., 25th Division

For Month of December 1917.

Volume XXVI.

WAR DIARY or INTELLIGENCE SUMMARY.

Army Form C. 2118.

Place	Date	Hour	Summary of Events and Information	Remarks and references to Appendices
GRUEPPE	Dec 1917. 1		Attended conference of A.D.V.S., I Corps who gave instructions re treatment of Ophthalmia as detailed in D.V.S. Circular Memo No 199.	/t
"	2		Inspected D.S.Q. and Signal Coy animals. Arranged for leaving of 4 sick in charge of Town Major, BOMY — 3 days rations supplied.	/t
"	3		Marched to WAVRANS to entrain for Third Army area.	/t
"	4		Detrained at ACHIET LE PETIT, marched to GREVILLERS.	/t
GREVILLERS			Handed over duties of A.D.V.S. to Major G.D. Norman, A.V.C.	

Forrest Capt/AC,
A.D.M.V.S., 25th Division.

WAR DIARY
or
INTELLIGENCE SUMMARY.
(Erase heading not required.)

Army Form C. 2118.

Place	Date	Hour	Summary of Events and Information	Remarks and references to Appendices
GREVILLERS	Dec 1917 5		DHQ moved from ACHIET LE PETIT to GREVILLERS	
"	6		Conference of V.Os and routine work. Inspected MVS and animals in Segregation Camp. Visit signed by and DHQ lines. Everything correct. In afternoon visited location of CCS re receiving animals for evacuation.	E.O.M.
"	7		Visited animals for evacuation also those in Segregation Camp. In company with the A.H. and Q.M.G. inspected 7th, 74th and 75th Inf. Bdes and accompanying M.G.Cs. and A.S.C. Coys. I found animals in good condition. and stable management very satisfactory. Very few sick. Shoeing and fodder also good. Animals of 1st Wilts not up to average, few in low condition. Veterinary equipment found complete. Routine and office work.	E.O.M.
"	8		Inspected horses in segregation, also visited 110th and 112th Bdes R.F.A.	E.O.M.
"	9		Veterinary equipment complete. Inspected Segregation Camp and DHQ units. Office routine. Perused office literature.	E.O.M.

Army Form C. 2118.

WAR DIARY
or
INTELLIGENCE SUMMARY.
(Erase heading not required.)

Place	Date Feb 1917	Hour	Summary of Events and Information	Remarks and references to Appendices
GREVILLERS	10		Inspected 7th Inf Bde. Found animals in good condition and well looked after, fodder being good. A few animals in M.G. Coy not up to average being rather poor. Advised keeping together and giving special diet. Visited FAVREUIL re prospective M.V.S. billet.	A.D.V.
"	11		Inspected Divisional Police horses and found them in very good condition. Inspected animals in Signalers Coy. also visited 76th Field Ambulance at BIHUCOURT and found everything correct.	A.D.V.
"	12		Visited 110th and 112th Bdes R.F.A. at FREMICOURT. Very few sick ones and animals in good condition, fodder good. Veterinary equipment complete.	A.D.V.
"	13		Visited D.H.Q. and inspected animals, forage and veterinary equipment. Also four trivial cases of sick. Stable management very good, animals being very fit. Fodder was good excepting some of the oats which were unfit for food. Weekly conference of V.Os.	A.D.V.
FAVREUIL	14		Visited ADMS, 3rd Division & inspected new billets of M.V.S etc. Moved into new quarters.	A.D.V.

Army Form C. 2118.

WAR DIARY
or
INTELLIGENCE SUMMARY.
(Erase heading not required.)

Instructions regarding War Diaries and Intelligence Summaries are contained in F.S. Regs., Part II. and the Staff Manual respectively. Title pages will be prepared in manuscript.

Place	Date	Hour	Summary of Events and Information	Remarks and references to Appendices
FAYREUIL	Dec 1917			
	15		Visited H.Q. South Staffords re incompency of during reported on same 16 "Q". Inspected animals in Segregation Camp also visited new position of 74th and 75th Inf. Bdes.	G.O.M.
"	16		Visited Segregation Camp and examined all areas. Attended conference of A.D.V.S. Corps.	G.O.M.
"	17		Visited 75th M.G. Coy and 75th Inf. Bde. Animals in good condition and satisfactory; no sick. Inspected Segregation Camp.	G.O.M.
"	18		Visited and inspected animals for evacuation also Segregation Camp. Inspected 112th Bde R.F.A. Two sick animals; horse management good.	G.O.M.
"	19		Visited 200 Coy A.S.C. and found everything correct. Inspected 25th M.A.C. and found everything correct; no sick; also visited M.V.S. Visited No. Coy Hqs Coy A.S.C.	G.O.M.
"	20		Visited and examined horses for evacuation and animals in Segregation. Conference of V.O.	G.O.M.

WAR DIARY
or
INTELLIGENCE SUMMARY.
(Erase heading not required.)

Army Form C. 2118.

Place	Date	Hour	Summary of Events and Information	Remarks and references to Appendices
FAYREUIL	21 Dec 1917		Visited animals in Signal Bn and Pioneers, also inspected the four Coys of Train and found everything correct. Very few sick; a few slight shrapnel wounds.	G.O.n.
"	22		Attended conference of A.D.V.S. Coys	G.O.n.
"	23		Inspected and examined animals in Segregation Camp. Visited and examined French Government horses at BIHUCOURT also Charger at AOHIET LE GRAND of IV Corps H.A. H.Q.	G.O.n.
"	24		Visited and examined animals in Segregation Camp and M.V.S.	G.O.n.
"	25		Visited MAC and examined 146 mules from Remounts. Visited M.V.S.	G.O.n.
"	26		Inspected 106 animals being transferred to outside units. Inspected animals of 74 R. Inf. Bde. Everything correct, sick nil.	G.O.n.
"	27		Visited M.V.S. and inspected animals for evacuation, also cases in Segregation. Conference of V.Os. in afternoon.	G.O.n.
"	28		Visited 12 R. Bty R.E. BAPAUME Inspected animals. Inspected 110-112 Bde R.F.A. Some of animals found in low condition. Stable management requires attention.	G.O.n.

Army Form C. 2118.

WAR DIARY
or
INTELLIGENCE SUMMARY.
(Erase heading not required.)

Place	Date	Hour	Summary of Events and Information	Remarks and references to Appendices
FAYREUIL	29		Attended conference of A.D.V.S., IV Corps. Visited and inspected animals in segregation.	E.M.
"	30		Inspected 166th Fd. Coy. R.E., 76th and 77th Field Ambs. Animals in good condition, very few sick. Visited M.V.S. also No.7 Army Troop Coy. R.E. Found animals in neglected condition, and lack of stable management.	E.M.
"	31		Visited M.V.S. and inspected animals for evacuation; also animals in segregation. Visited 125 M.G. Coy. and inspected animals. Found everything correct, sick nil.	E.M.

Confidential

War Diary

of

Major G.D. Norman, A.V.C.

D.A.D.V.S., 35th Division.

From Jan 1st 1918 to Jan 31st 1918.

Volume XXVIII

WAR DIARY
or
INTELLIGENCE SUMMARY.
(Erase heading not required.)

Army Form C. 2118.

Place	Date	Hour	Summary of Events and Information	Remarks and references to Appendices
FAVREUIL	JAN. 1918			
	1		Visited and inspected animals in Sapignies Camp. Inspected 75th Field Amb. Stable management very good; sick nil. Also visited 12th Field Coy R.E. Grooming slack and horses' condition needed improvement.	G.O.M.
	2		Visited 76th Field Amb. inspected animals. Condition good and sick nil. Inspected animals for evacuation at M.V.S.	G.O.M.
	3		Visited 198 Coy A.S.C. Condition and stable management very good; also visited No 2 Section of D.A.C. Inspected animals in Sapignies Camp.	G.O.M.
	4		Visited and inspected 74th Inf. Bde. also 106th Field Coy R.E. Animals in each, condition good and grooming generally good. Forage good, and watering equipment conforms. Visited animals in M.V.S. and Sapignies Camp.	G.O.M.
	5		Attended conference of A.D.V.S. IV Corps. Visited M.V.S. and inspected animals.	G.O.M.
	6		Visited 12th Field Coy R.E. re sick. Inspected lines. Stable management good. Two animals sent to M.V.S. Visited R.T.O., BAPAUME re evacuation of sick and mule autopsy arrangements.	G.O.M.
	7		Inspected remounts and distribution of same. Visited and inspected animals in	G.O.M.

WAR DIARY
or
INTELLIGENCE SUMMARY.
(Erase heading not required.)

Army Form C. 2118.

Place	Date JAN 1918	Hour	Summary of Events and Information	Remarks and references to Appendices
FAVREUIL	7 (cont)		M.V.S. for evacuation, also cases in Segregation Camp. Visited and inspected E.V.Cs. charges.	G.O.R.
"	8		Visited M.V.S. and examined animals in lines also animals in Segregation Camp.	G.O.R.
			In BAPAUME inspecting horse ambulance and arranged to take it.	
"	9		Inspected 7th Inf. Bde. Grooming and stable management gd. Side practically nil, and found receiving equipment correct. Visited M.V.S.	G.O.R.
"	10		Sick and mange sent to 75th Gild. Awt. returning for light duty only on the 15th.	G.O.R.
"	16		Met Capt JONES, A.V.C. Army Vety on my absence.	G.O.R.
"	17		Office routine and clearing up papers and notes. Visited M.V.S. and inspected huts, equipment and lines. Room hut required.	G.O.R.
"			Clearing substation paid to inspection. Inspected animals in segregation. Held conference of Officers.	G.O.R.
"	12		Visited and inspected 110 H. Bde. R.F.A. "C and D" Batteries very good. "B" Battery required attention in grooming and stablemanagement. Also "A" Battery, Vets being prevalent. Inspected receiving equipment installed and incomplete ("C" Battery). Visited 7th Army Troops Coy R.E. (Royal Monmouth Engineers) and found animals improved.	G.O.R.

Army Form C. 2118.

WAR DIARY
or
INTELLIGENCE SUMMARY.
(Erase heading not required.)

(3)

Instructions regarding War Diaries and Intelligence Summaries are contained in F. S. Regs., Part II. and the Staff Manual respectively. Title pages will be prepared in manuscript.

Place	Date	Hour	Summary of Events and Information	Remarks and references to Appendices
	JAN 1918			
FAVREUIL	19		Attended conference of A.D.V.S., IV Corps. Visited 76th Field Amb. and inspected animals and lines.	F.M.
"	20		Inspected 112th Bde R.F.A. and found animals looking well and stablemanagement good. On sick and veterinary equipment complete: also inspected 4th South Staffords and 7th M.G. Coy. South Staffords in fair condition. Some animals of M.G. Coy. needed attention, being rather poor.	F.M.
"	21		Visited and inspected 195 M.G. Coy and found everything in order. Mules in good condition and well stabled. Visited and inspected animals for evacuation, also those under treatment in segregation. Appointed President of Court of Enquiry to loss of French Mules Royale.	F.M.
"	22		Visited A.D.V.S. Corps on duty; also inspected animals in Segregation Camp.	F.M.
"	23		Visited 76th Field Amb. and inspected animals etc. Everything in good order, no sick. Also inspected 195th M.G. Coy animals and lines. Visited M.V.S.	F.M.
"	24		Visited M.V.S. and examined animals for evacuation. Inspected 106 & 130 Field Coys R.E. and 110 Sqdn. Officers' chargers in 106th Field Coy R.E. require attention in grooming and exercise etc. Held conference of V.Os.	F.M.

Army Form C. 2118.

WAR DIARY
or
INTELLIGENCE SUMMARY.

(Erase heading not required.)

Instructions regarding War Diaries and Intelligence Summaries are contained in F. S. Regs., Part II. and the Staff Manual respectively. Title pages will be prepared in manuscript.

Place	Date JAN	Hour	Summary of Events and Information	Remarks and references to Appendices
FAYREUIL	25		Visited No 1 and 2 Sectns D.A.C. and found everything correct. No 1 Sectn still in the open, and animals gone back. Visited S.V. Bordens (Pioneers), animals very good, also visited M.V.S.	
"	26		Attended conference of A.D.V.S., IV Corps. Visited and examined M.V.S. and animals in segregation.	E.A.M.
"	27		Visited and inspected 75th # mangel mungels at supply officer re issue. Also inspected 198 Coy A.S.C. Animals' condition good, and sick nil, excepting two cases of Ophthalmia (evacuated). Visited and inspected Police Horses.	E.A.M.
"	28		Visited M.V.S. and inspected animals ft evacuation, also camp. Visited No 2 Sectn D.A.C. and D Batty 112th Bde. Found everything in order.	E.A.M.
"	29		Visited 199 Coy A.S.C. re bombing and injured animals; also visit in afternoon re culling of skins and fats. Visited M.V.S. and 75th Field Amb.	E.A.M.
"	30		Visit to 199 Coy A.S.C. re casualties from bomb also visited 75th and 77th Field Amb. Attended Lecture by Rev. B. Bouchier, also visited M.V.S.	E.A.M.
"	31		Visited and inspected 75th D.I. Bde. Everything in order except horses of 2nd S Lancs which were in poor condition. Visited M.V.S. re evacuation. Held conference of V.Os.	E.A.M.

D.A.D.V.S.,
25TH DIVISION.
No. 1/3/1918
Date.......

Vol 29

Confidential

War Diary

of

Major G.D. Norman, A.V.C.,

D.A.D.V.S., 25th Division.

From Feb 1st 1918 to Feb 28th 1918.

Volume XXIX

ORIGINAL

Army Form C. 2118.

WAR DIARY
or
INTELLIGENCE SUMMARY.
(Erase heading not required.)

Instructions regarding War Diaries and Intelligence Summaries are contained in F. S. Regs., Part II. and the Staff Manual respectively. Title pages will be prepared in manuscript.

Place	Date	Hour	Summary of Events and Information	Remarks and references to Appendices
FAKREUIL	FEB 1918			
	1		Visited 2nd South Lancs also the M.V.S. Inspected 70/ Coy D.A.C. Animals much improved by being in stables. Sick Nil and sty equipment complete.	E.M.
"	2		Examined animals in Syrington Camp. Attended conference of A.D.V.S, IV Corps.	E.M.
"	3		Inspected air drain and found animals in good order. Stable guard also veterinary equipment complete. Inspected remounts before distribution.	E.M.
"	4		Visited M.V.S and inspected animals for evacuation and animals in recuperation.	E.M.
"	5		Visited 76th Field Amb. Stable management good. Sick nil. Visited 2nd South Lancs, South Staffords, and Gunners, also visited 199 Coy A.S.C and examined remounts.	E.M.
"	6		Inspected 76th Field Amb. Found everything in good order. Visited M.V.S and examined camps etc., also Q.R., 49th and 150th Labour Corps.	E.M.
"	7		Visited 74th Inf Bde for inspection with Brig General Commanding (who did not attend). Everything in good order. Held conference of V.Os in afternoon.	E.M.
"	8		Visited 74th Inf Bde and examined several animals in company with Brigadier re evacuating and transferring to Remounts. Visited Police Horses and operated on one animal with deep arm wound.	E.M.

T2134. Wt. W708—776. 500000. 4/15. Sir J. C. & S.

Army Form C. 2118.

WAR DIARY
or
INTELLIGENCE SUMMARY.
(Erase heading not required.)

Instructions regarding War Diaries and Intelligence Summaries are contained in F.S. Regs., Part II. and the Staff Manual respectively. Title pages will be prepared in manuscript.

Place	Date FEB 1918	Hour	Summary of Events and Information	Remarks and references to Appendices
FAVREUIL	9		Attended conference of A.D.V.S., IV Corps. Visited ACHIET LE GRAND re transfer of 51st Divisional M.V.S. to us. Visited 76th Field Amb.	E.M.
"	10		Visited M.V.S. and examined animals in camp and those in segregation.	E.M.
"	11		Went to ACHIET re position of M.V.S. Also visited 19th and 200 Corps A.S.C.	E.M.
"	12		Visited M.V.S.	E.M.
"	13		Visited COURCELLES and ACHIET LE PETIT re finding site for M.V.S. Visited A.D.V.S., IV Corps on Mty.	E.M.
ACHIET LE PETIT	13		Division moved to ACHIET area.	E.M.
"	14		Inspected remounts point of distribution. Visited LOGEAST WOOD re site for M.V.S. Held conference of V.Os.	E.M.
"	15		Visited M.V.S. and examined animals for encounter. Inspected 4th Sptk.	E.M.
"	16		Staff duties at COURCELLES and new site for M.V.S. Attended conference of A.D.V.S. IV Corps. Visited M.G. Battalion and Pioneers.	E.M.
"	17		Visited 130th Field Coy R.E. and 76th Field Amb. Visited M.V.S. re plan of camp etc, and fixing up labour etc.	E.M.

WAR DIARY
or
INTELLIGENCE SUMMARY.
(Erase heading not required.)

Army Form C. 2118.

Place	Date FEB 1918	Hour	Summary of Events and Information	Remarks and references to Appendices
ACHIET LE PETIT	18		A.D.V.S. IV Corps visited Division and inspected M.V.S, 76th Field Amb, 77th Field Amb, and 130th Field Coy R.E. I visited H.Q. and No.1 Section D.A.C. and found everything in order.	E.M.
"	19		Visited M.V.S and 130th Field Coy R.E. re instruction of camp also examined animals for evacuation. Visited Nos 2 and 3 Sections DAC in BAPAUME.	E.M.
"	20		Visited 25th Divisional M.G. Battalion, and inspected 199, 200, and 201 Coys	E.M.
"	21		of the Train. Inspected M.V.S. Inspected 110th, 116th R.F.A at BOUZINCOURT also 196 By A.S.C. Also visited and inspected 112th, 116th R.F.A at MEAULTE in company with A.D.V.S., IV Corps. Found stable management and animals good. Very few sick. On returning equipment was complete and well kept.	E.M.
"	22		Visited M.V.S. and inspected camp and animals in segregation. Inspected and reported on G.O.C's charger. Visited 4th South Staffords at COURCELLES	E.M.
"	23		Attended conference of A.D.V.S., IV Corps, and Remount Holding Parade with D.D. Remounts, Third Army in afternoon.	E.M.

Army Form C. 2118.

WAR DIARY
or
INTELLIGENCE SUMMARY.
(Erase heading not required.)

Instructions regarding War Diaries and Intelligence Summaries are contained in F.S. Regs., Part II. and the Staff Manual respectively. Title pages will be prepared in manuscript.

Place	Date	Hour	Summary of Events and Information	Remarks and references to Appendices
ACHIET LE PETIT	Feb. 1918 24		Visited M.G. Corps, 3rd Worcesters, and 6th S.W.B.(Pioneers), and inspected animals. Everything in good order. Assisted G.O.C. in judging transport of M.G. Battalion in afternoon.	J. DN.
"	25		Visited M.V.S. and examined animals in respiration. Also killing of his etc. Visited 75.R 76R 7F.O. and inspected B.R. Border and Scots Lancs. Found everything in order.	J. DN.
"	26		Visited A.D.V.S. IV Corps in morning, also M.V.S. re erection of stables meeting R.E. officer.	J. DN.
"	27		Made enquiries re one of Strizootic Lymphangitis reported as being evacuated from 37 M.V.S. on 12.2.1918. This was a remount received by 100 Coy A.S.C. from DIEPPE on 3-2-1918. On arrival it showed an ill naturally enthused wound on the shoulder with no discharge. It was regripped, branded, and sent to M.V.S. Later. No lymphatic lesions were apparent on observed. All animals of unit examined and found free from mange and quite healthy. Growing hit reclothing of animal trunk. Sent reports to 17 D.V.S. IV Corps etc.	J. DN.
"	28		Visited M.V.S. and inspected sick animals in respiration, also killing of camp. Proceeded on leave from March 1st to 15 R.	J. DN.

Joined B.E.F. 26-9-15.

Vol 30

Confidential.

War Diary

of

Major G.D. Norman, A.V.C.

D.A.D.V.S., 25th Division

From March 1st 1918 to March 31st 1918

Volume XXX

WAR DIARY
or
INTELLIGENCE SUMMARY.
(Erase heading not required.)

Army Form C. 2118.

Instructions regarding War Diaries and Intelligence Summaries are contained in F. S. Regs., Part II. and the Staff Manual respectively. Title pages will be prepared in manuscript.

Place	Date	Hour	Summary of Events and Information	Remarks and references to Appendices
ACHIET LE PETIT	MARCH 1918			
	1		Inspected 7th Inf. Bde., T-Train, 25th Bn. M.G.C. 74th Inf. Bde. and 105th Field	
"	2		Cof R.E. Attended conference of A.D.V.S. IV Corps. Elected fresh comp. of 199 Cof H.S.C.	
"	3		Inspected 75th Field Amb., 108th Field Cof RE and 25th Div. Train. Visited 25th Bn. M.G.C. re 8 surplus animals. Set 2 S MVS. 2 S. TSO. Signals and one arriving remounts.	
"	4		Inspected 7 + 74 Inf. Bdes. Visited MVS re case of suspected Epizootic Alluritis	
"	5		inspected. Inspected 149 A.M. Coy HSC, DHQ and Signals	
"	6		Inspected 108 Field Cof RE and 75th Field Amb. Visited MVS	
"	7		Inspected 25th Div Train and 25th Signal Cof	
"	8		Conference for execution veterinary stores. Inspected 25th Bn. M.G.C. 7+74 Inf. Bdes. 75th Field Amb. and 105 TOC Field Cof	
			R.E.	
"	9		Attended conference of A.D.V.S. IV Corps. Inspected 25th Div Train	
"	10		Inspected remounts, 1st Wilts. T.M.O., 7th Inf. Bde., 105th Field Cof RE and 200 Cof H.S.C.	
			Increase of mange 3 outfits.	

WAR DIARY
or
INTELLIGENCE SUMMARY.
(Erase heading not required.)

Army Form C. 2118.

Place	Date	Hour	Summary of Events and Information	Remarks and references to Appendices
ACHIET-LE-PETIT	March 1917	11	Inspected 7th Inf. Bde. A.S.O, 106th Field Amb. R.E. 75th Bull Amb, and animals for evacuation in M.V.S.	
"		12	Inspected 25th Div. Train, M.G. Bn and 10th Cheshires	
"		13	Inspected 75th Inf. Bde, D.H.Q and visited M.V.S.	
"		14	Conference for T.Os. Inspected 198 Coy A.S.C.	
"		15	Inspected 25 Div M.P. Transport Coy, M.G. Tentr, 7th Inf Bde, 105th Field Coy R.E. and 25th Div. Train	
"		16	Returned from leave after being devised a day at BOULOGNE	E.O.M.
"		17	Visited 198 and 200 Coys A.S.C. inspected animals re suspected mange.	E.O.M.
"		18	Inspected M.V.S. animals and Camp. Found everything in order. Visited 1st Wilts, 4th Suth Stafford. and 6th S.W.B. (Pioneers) Inspected animals and lines and found everything correct. Visited lines camp of S.W.Bs re rank of Lieut M. 8.3.18 and reprimanded same to G.O.C.	
"		19	Visited M.V.S. and inspected animals in aggregation and for evacuation. Visited D.A.C. found animals in good condition and well worked.	E.O.M.

WAR DIARY
or
INTELLIGENCE SUMMARY.
(Erase heading not required.)

Army Form C. 2118.

Place	Date March 1918	Hour	Summary of Events and Information	Remarks and references to Appendices
ACHIET LE PETIT	20		Visited 6.S.W.B. (Pioneers) and Div. Pack Transport Coy. also A and C Coy # M.G. Batn. Also an A.D.V.S. IV Corps on turning in. A.D.V.S. IV Corps came in afternoon for inspection of M.V.S. & accompanied him.	E.M.
"	21		Whole offensive began and Division ordered to be all day. Visited M.V.S. fire during day. We arranging for sick to be left with Area Commandant at Achene of V.B.	E.M.
"	22		Visited M.V.S. evacuated animals to evacuation. Visited A.D.V.S. IV Corps with D.A.D.V.S. 6th Division. M.V.Ss. fired through Arrived P.st at BIENVILLERS etc. Standing to all day.	E.M.
"	23		Prepared to move M.V.S. moved to BUCQUOY. Travelled M.V.S. fire and went to MIRAUMONT to ascertain risk.	E.M.
"	24		D.H.Q. moved to billet of Train in BUCQUOY-RD.	E.M.
PUISEAUX	25		D.H.Q. moved to PUISEAUX and M.V.S. to HANNESCAMPS	E.M.
FONQUEVILLERS	26		D.H.Q. moved to FONQUEVILLERS. M.V.S. to AUTHIE. Visited A.D.V.S. IV Corps at MARIEUX	E.M.
POMMIER	27		D.H.Q. to POMMIER Visited M.V.S. at AUTHEUILE and finally to CANAPLES filled with M.V.S.	E.M.

WAR DIARY
or
INTELLIGENCE SUMMARY.

Army Form C. 2118.

Place	Date	Hour	Summary of Events and Information	Remarks and references to Appendices
BERNEUIL	28 Nov 1915		Staff with MYS at CANAPLES. Visited DHQ at BERNEUIL and took arrangements to learn work with Cavalry MYS.	F.M.
"	30		Visited 169 ASC, AA Scott Supports and 7th Fld HQ. Visited MYS and stayed with same at CANAPLES	F.M.
"	31		Travelled to CANDAS for entraining.	F.M.

Joined B.E.F. 26-9-1915.

VA 31

Confidential

War Diary

of

Major G.D Norman, A.V.C.

D.A.D.V.S. 25th Division

for Month of April 1918

Volume XXXI

26

Original

WAR DIARY
or
INTELLIGENCE SUMMARY.
(Erase heading not required)

Army Form C. 2118.

Place	Date	Hour	Summary of Events and Information	Remarks and references to Appendices
MERRIS	APRIL 1918			
	1		Entrained at CANDAS arr 6 MVS for CAESTRE and marched to BAILLEUL Staph.	
			Night with MVS at BULLER LINES.	G.M.
"	2		Joined DHQ at MERRIS. Visited DADVS, 2nd Australian Division at	
			RAVELSBERG re taking over. Camp foot MVS. Visited MVS and inspected animals	G.M.
			+ Camp etc. Visited sick and units at MERRIS.	G.M.
RAVELSBERG	3		Moved camp to RAVELSBERG. Visited MVS. Attended sale at D.H.Q.	G.M.
"	4		Visited MVS and DADVS, 9th Division re evacuation of large from	
			BAC ST MAUR. Conference of VOs in afternoon	G.M.
"	5		Visited 199. 201 + 201 Coys A.S.C. and inspected lines. Animals good	
			order and few sick. also visited MG Batts. DHQ Signals and 77th R Field	
			Amb in afternoon	G.M.
"	6		Attended conference of A.D.V.S., IX Corps at FLETRE. Visited MVS.	G.M.
			inspected camp and animals in sick lines.	
"	7		Inspected 7th Inf. Bde also 105. 1/20 Field Coys RE. Few sick and	
			animals well rated etc. Visited QQC, 75 R Bde re requisition for changes &	G.M.
"	8		Visited MVS. Examined animals in suspicion sick lines.	G.M.

Army Form C. 2118.

WAR DIARY
or
INTELLIGENCE SUMMARY.
(Erase heading not required.)

Instructions regarding War Diaries and Intelligence Summaries are contained in F. S. Regs., Part II. and the Staff Manual respectively. Title pages will be prepared in manuscript.

Place	Date April 1918	Hour	Summary of Events and Information	Remarks and references to Appendices
RAVELSBERG	8	(cont)	Visited D.A.D.V.S, 19th Division re evacuation of camp.	G.M.
"	9		Visited 76th Field Amb. and 200 Coy A.S.C. Found everything correct and	G.M.
			for sick.	
"	10		Journeyed to METEREN & M.V.S. which had moved from BULLER LINES M.V.S. had meanwhile been attached to KRUYSTRAETE near GODEWAERSVELDE.	G.M.
			Returned to DHQ. Spending to afternoon and all night.	G.M.
"	11		Journeyed to M.V.S. KRUYSTRAETE and remained there. Visited Div Train.	G.M.
"	12		Inspected animals for evacuation to ST OMER	G.M.
			Moved with M.V.S. from KRUYSTRAETE to STEENVOORDE	G.M.
STEENVOORDE	13			G.M.
"	14		Inspected 25th D.A.C.	
			Visited DHQ at BOESCHEPE and received G.O.C's orders re visits	G.M.
BOESCHEPE	15			
"	16		75th Field Amb, 7th Inf Bde. Hosp. for evacuation etc.	
			Visited DHQ at BOESCHEPE and arranged re issuing of remounts and steps.	G.M.
"	17		Inspected and used St-remounts to units	G.M.
			Inspected animals for evacuation and visited 77th Field Amb and	
			M.G. Battalion.	G.M.

Army Form C. 2118.

WAR DIARY
or
INTELLIGENCE SUMMARY.
(Erase heading not required.)

Instructions regarding War Diaries and Intelligence Summaries are contained in F. S. Regs., Part II. and the Staff Manual respectively. Title pages will be prepared in manuscript.

(3)

Place	Date April 1918	Hour	Summary of Events and Information	Remarks and references to Appendices
BOESCHEPE	18		Journey to D.H.Q. near BOESCHEPE and attempt to requisition for remounts	G.M.
STEENVOORDE			Visited near D.H.Q. at STEENVOORDE. Visited to DAC re remounts.	
"	19		Visited D.H.Q. also Div. train and 75th Inf. Bde. Received visit from A.D.V.S., IX Corps.	G.M.
"	20		Attended conference at IX Corps. Visited 7th Inf. Bde and M.G. Battalion. Inspected animals for evacuation.	G.M.
"	21		Visited D.H.Q. at STEENVOORDE. D.H.Q. moved to COUTHOVE Château.	G.M.
COUTHOVE Château			(between POPERINGHE and PROVEN) Moved with M.V.S. to Mounted Camp 4 Km. N. of POPERINGHE.	G.M.
27.F.21.a.	22		Visited 7th Inf. Bde and inspected animals. Moved to D.H.Q. and fixed up office and billet.	G.M.
"	23		Visited M.V.S. in new camp at HAMHOEK. Inspected animals for evacuation. Those in apparatus etc. Animals sick remained D.H.Q.	G.M.
"	24		Visited J.H.Q. Signals, 106 R.M.G.R.E., 130 R. Z. G.Y. RE and 4th South Staffords. Found the animals in fair condition and healthy. There were few sick and the vety equipment was attended to. Attended sick animals at D.H.Q.	G.M.

WAR DIARY
or
INTELLIGENCE SUMMARY.
(Erase heading not required.)

Army Form C. 2118.

Place	Date April 1918	Hour	Summary of Events and Information	Remarks and references to Appendices
COUTHOVE Chateau	25		Inspected 25th Div Train tew 198 Coy A.S.C. Found animals healthy & in good condition. Standing to after mid-day.	G.M.
	26		Standing to all day. Visited 75th Inf. Bde and examined transport.	G.M.
	27		Journeyed to WATOU and inspected 6th S.W.B. (Pioneers) attached sick cases at D.H.Q. Visited 130 Fd Coy R.E.	G.M.
	28		Visited M.V.S. at WIPPENHOEK, rank arranged for its removal to WATOU neighbourhood.	G.M.
	29		Journeyed to M.V.S. and inspected animals ranks etc. Visited 7th Inf Bde and found everything correct, also visited 199 Coy r 201 Coy A.S.C. Journeyed to M.V.S. inspected animals. Arranged for more to	G.M.
	30		Couction west of STEENVOORDE. Attended sick animals at D.H.Q.	G.M.

Joined B.E.F. 26-9-1915.

Vol 32

Confidential

War Diary

of

Major G.D. Norman, A.V.C.

D.A.D.V.S., 25th Division

From May 1st 1918 To May 31st 1918

Volume XXXII

2]
Original

Army Form C. 2118.

WAR DIARY
or
INTELLIGENCE SUMMARY.
(Erase heading not required.)

Instructions regarding War Diaries and Intelligence Summaries are contained in F. S. Regs., Part II. and the Staff Manual respectively. Title pages will be prepared in manuscript.

Place	Date May 1918	Hour	Summary of Events and Information	Remarks and references to Appendices
COUTHOVE CHATEAU	1		Inspected 319th Roads Construction Coy and 30th Labour Group. Visited M.V.S. at new location 27.K.21.d.9.9. also 109, 200 & 201 Coys A.S.C.	G.D.M.
"	2		Inspected 74th and 75th Inf. Bdes. Found animals in fair condition and very few sick. Veterinary equipment in good order. Held conference of V.Os.	G.D.M.
"	3		Inspected 7th Inf. Bde. Animals in good condition and veterinary equipment complete. Visited M.V.S. and inspected animals for evacuation, also saw the transport of S.A.A. Sectn D.A.C.	G.D.M.
BAMBECQUE	4		D.H.Q. moved from COUTHOVE Chateau to BAMBECQUE. Visited M.V.S and inspected animals and camp etc, also visited 198 Coy A.S.C.	G.D.M.
"	5			G.D.M.
"	6		Held court on two men of M.V.S. charged with being drunk etc. Journeyed to HOUTKERQUE and also visited 75th Field Amb.	G.D.M.
"	7		Inspected Signals, 105, 106 & 130 & Coys R.E., also visited M.V.S. re evacuation of horses.	G.D.M.
"	8		D.H.Q. entrained travelled to ARCIS LE PONSART coming under IX Corps. arriving there on 11th inst.	G.D.M.

Army Form C. 2118.

WAR DIARY
or
INTELLIGENCE SUMMARY.

(Erase heading not required.)

Instructions regarding War Diaries and Intelligence Summaries are contained in F. S. Regs., Part II. and the Staff Manual respectively. Title pages will be prepared in manuscript.

Place	Date MAY 1918	Hour	Summary of Events and Information	Remarks and references to Appendices
ARCIS-LE	12		Inspected 75th Inf. Bde, 76th Bde and 1/200 Coy A.S.C.	G.O.M.
BONGART	13		Journeyed to 110 Bde R.F.A. also to 110 R. Bde R.F.A. at UNCHAIR and 105 R. Bde R.F.A. Animals in fair condition excepting "A" Battery. Found veterinary equipment complete and in good order. Inspected M.V.S.	G.O.M.
"	14		Inspected D.A.C. at COHAN and 198 Coy A.S.C. at VIZELLY.	G.O.M.
"	15		Inspected 112th Bde R.F.A. at BROUILLET and inspected death of three animals from poisoning. Inspected 2nd Scots Lancs at ST GILLES at request of G.O.C. Visited M.V.S. Inspected camp animals in reception.	G.O.M.
"	16		Received visit from A.D.V.S., X Corps who inspected M.V.S. etc.	G.O.M.
"	17		Visited Reinforcement Camp at COHAN. Held conference of V.Os. Journeyed to GRUGNY and examined men at Divisional Wing re fitness as transport drivers.	G.O.M.
"	18		Attended conference of A.D.V.S. Corps at MONTIGNY.	G.O.M.
"	19		Visited M.V.S. Inspected camp and animals in reception, also inspected S.A.A. Section D.A.C. Found everything in good order.	G.O.M.
"	20		Inspected 110 R. Bde R.F.A. at UNCHAIR, especially "A" Battery re outbreak of	

Army Form C. 2118.

WAR DIARY
or
INTELLIGENCE SUMMARY.
(Erase heading not required.)

Place	Date	Hour	Summary of Events and Information	Remarks and references to Appendices
	MAY 1918			
ARCIS LE PONSART	21		Enigma Ryokenpitsi. Inspected M.G. Bath and 109 Coy A.S.C. Some of M.G.Bn animals in low condition; otherwise good. Test equipment required making up.	G.O.M.
"	22		Inspected 74th Inf Bde and S.W.B. (Pioneer). Animals well kept except mules of North Lancs. Many animals in low condition.	G.O.M.
MONTIGNY	23		Inspected animal rest camp of M.V.S. D.H.Q. moved from ARCIS LE PONSART to MONTIGNY.	G.O.M.
"	24		Found suitable camp for M.V.S. Inspected D.A.C. at BASUEUX and arranged for V.O. to live with 110 & 73rd Bde R.F.A. temporarily.	G.O.M.
"	25		Attended conference of A.D.V.S., X Corps. Visited M.V.S. and examined animals in camp.	G.O.M.
"	26		Inspected 165, 106 M. Coys R.E. and 4 th South Staffords.	G.O.M.
ARCIS LE PONSART	27		D.H.Q moved to ARCIS LE PONSART. German attack began at dawn.	G.O.M.
GOUZINCOURT	28		D.H.Q moved to GOUZINCOURT	G.O.M.
LA CHAPELLE	29		D.H.Q moved via PASSY to VERNEUIL, chapel outside S. of MARNE and moved in evening to LA CHAPELLE	G.O.M.

Army Form C. 2118.

WAR DIARY
or
INTELLIGENCE SUMMARY.
(Erase heading not required.)

(4)

Instructions regarding War Diaries and Intelligence Summaries are contained in F. S. Regs., Part II. and the Staff Manual respectively. Title pages will be prepared in manuscript.

Place	Date	Hour	Summary of Events and Information	Remarks and references to Appendices
	MAY 1918			
LaCHAPELLE	30		Visited 76th Field Amb. and 112th 113th R.F.A. DHQ left in evening for BERGERES and arrived there on 31st inst.	G.O.M.
BERGERES	31		Arrived at BERGERES about 1 P.M. Fixed up and opened office etc.	G.O.M.

Confidential.

War Diary

of

Major G. D. Nasmith, A.V.C.,

D.A.D.V.S., 25th Division.

From June 1st 1918 to June 20th 1918.

Volume XXXIII

Army Form C. 2118.

WAR DIARY
or
INTELLIGENCE SUMMARY.
(Erase heading not required.)

Instructions regarding War Diaries and Intelligence Summaries are contained in F. S. Regs., Part II. and the Staff Manual respectively. Title pages will be prepared in manuscript.

Place	Date June 1918	Hour	Summary of Events and Information	Remarks and references to Appendices
BERGERES	1		Attended conference at Oulchy also visited 110th Bde R.F.A. at COHIGNY re animals affected with Epizootic Lymphangitis.	A.S.V.4
"	2		Journeyed to LOISY and inspected 75th Infy Bde also No 1 + 2 Sections D.A.C.	A.S.V.4a
ETOGES	3		D.H.Q. moved from BERGERES to ETOGES. Moved in advance and arranged camp for M.V.S.	A.S.V.4b
"	4		Visited M.V.S. re received animals. Visited 110th Bde R.F.A. re vegetation disinfection of A.T Battery re case of Epizootic Lymphangitis. Inspected M.G. Battalion.	A.S.V.4
"	5		Inspected 199 Coy A.S.C. and 7th Infy Bde. Everything in order. Few sick.	A.S.V.4
"	6		Inspected 74th Infy Bde. Animals generally improved and few casualties.	A.S.V.4a
"	7		Inspected 2ovoCoy A.S.C. Animals in good order. Held conference of V.Os. Journeyed to LOISY inspected animals of 75th Infy Bde. Found animals in good condition. Owing of 2nd South Brics very bad; suggested urgent attention to same. Examined animals in M.V.S.	A.S.V.4
"	8		Attended conference at VERTUS. Visited H.Q. Signals.	A.S.V.4
ALLEMANT	9		D.H.Q. moved from ETOGES to ALLEMANT	A.S.V.4
"	10		Visited 75th Infy Bde at ST LOUP 2nd Coy A.S.C, S.W.B. and 76th Field Ambulance.	A.S.V.4

WAR DIARY
or
INTELLIGENCE SUMMARY.

Army Form C. 2118.

Place	Date	Hour	Summary of Events and Information	Remarks and references to Appendices
ALLEMANT	JUNE 1918 11		Visited R.F.A details at OYES including No.1 Section D.A.C. also visited 74th Inf Bde at ZOEUVRES. A.D.V.S Corps visited 37 M.V.S.	A.S.24
	12		Visited R.F.A at OYES and D.A.C, also saw V.O re suspected mange cases.	A.S.24
	13		Visited M.G Batts and inspected animals. Received visit from A.D.V.S Corps and visited 75th Inf Bde Lorry finding animals in good condition with few sick.	A.S.24
PLEURS	14		D.H.Q moved from ALLEMANT to PLEURS. Inspected M.G Battalion with O.C Train	A.S.24
"	15		Attended conference at Corps	A.S.24
"	16		Accompanied A.D.V.S Corps on his inspection of Artillery and 106th Field Amb R.E. Attendance to sick animals of H.Q units.	A.S.24
"	17		Visited 75th Bde Lorry at ST LOUP also M.V.S at ALLEMANT	A.S.24
"	18		Journeyed to GAYINCHY and GAYE inspected 74th Bde Lorry, also went to SEZANNE to see animals slaughtered for food	A.S.24
"	19		Visited M.V.S inspected animals for evacuation. Visited Train Corps with O.C Train	A.S.24

WAR DIARY
or
INTELLIGENCE SUMMARY.
(Erase heading not required.)

Army Form C. 2118.

Place	Date 1918	Hour	Summary of Events and Information	Remarks and references to Appendices
FLEURS	JUNE 20		Journey to OGNES and CORBOY and inspected D.A.C, 110th T&M R.F.A, B/112th Bde and M.G. Battn.	A.S.V.4
"	21		Held conference F.V.O. visited 105th Fd.Cy R.E. and 3rd Worcesters	A.S.V.4
"	22		Attended conference of A.D.V.S. Corps, also visited M.V.S. inspected M.H.S. and animals for evacuation.	A.S.V.4
"	23		Visited 105th Fd. Cy R.E. Krimpelpost needed extra attention.	A.S.V.4
"	24		Inspected 75th Bde Group	A.S.V.4
"	25		Inspected animals at D.H.Q Signal Cy, also visited M.V.S. Division entrained at MAILLY and proceeded to ROYON detraining at MARESQUE. An Ro. 27th inst.	A.S.V.4
ROYON	28 29 30		Inspection of M.V.S. H.Q, Division Signal Coy. Office routine and handing over of administrative duties to O.C, M.V.S. as D.H.Q. is to proceed to England.	A.S.V.4

Joined B.E.F. 26-9-15

VOL 24

Confidential

War Diary

of

Major G.D. Norman, A.V.C.

D.A.D.V.S., 25th Division

From July 1st 1918 to July 31st 1918.

Volume XXXIV.

Army Form C. 2118.

WAR DIARY
or
INTELLIGENCE SUMMARY.
(Erase heading not required.)

Instructions regarding War Diaries and Intelligence Summaries are contained in F. S. Regs., Part II. and the Staff Manual respectively. Title pages will be prepared in manuscript.

Place	Date July 1918	Hour	Summary of Events and Information	Remarks and references to Appendices
ALDERSHOT	1-9		Office work and return.	G.O.R.
"	10		Inspecting stables at Aurelian Camp.	G.O.R.
"	11		Visited Remount Depôt Aldershot and inspected 12 ration period.	
			to their issue to Division.	G.O.R.
"	12		Inspected animals at Aurelian Camp.	G.O.R.
"	13 / 31		General Routine office work.	G.O.R.

Confidential.

War Diary.
of
Major G. D. Norman, A.V.C.
D.A.D.V.S., 25th Division.
From Aug 1st 1918 to Aug 31st 1918.

Volume XXXV

Army Form C. 2118.

WAR DIARY
or
INTELLIGENCE SUMMARY.
(Erase heading not required.)

Place	Date	Hour	Summary of Events and Information	Remarks and references to Appendices
ALDERSHOT	Aug 1st to 31st 1918.		Nothing of special interest to report.	F.D.M.

Confidential
War Diary

of

Major G.D. Norman, A.V.C.

D.A.D.V.S., 25th Division

from the month of

September 1918

Volume XXXVI

Army Form C. 2118.

WAR DIARY
or
INTELLIGENCE SUMMARY.

(Erase heading not required.)

Instructions regarding War Diaries and Intelligence Summaries are contained in F. S. Regs., Part II. and the Staff Manual respectively. Title pages will be prepared in manuscript.

Place	Date	Hour	Summary of Events and Information	Remarks and references to Appendices

WAR DIARY
or
INTELLIGENCE SUMMARY.

Army Form C. 2118.

Place	Date	Hour	Summary of Events and Information	Remarks and references to Appendices
ALDERSHOT	Sept. 1918 1-14		Nothing of special interest to report.	G.O.M.
	14		Left ALDERSHOT for FRANCE	G.O.M.
	16		Arrived at ST. RIQUIER	G.O.M.
ST RIQUIER	17		Routine work at office. Visited M.V.S at	G.O.M.
	18		Visited 7th Inf. Bde. 2nd & 21st Manchester, 9th & Newtns (5th)	G.O.M.
			Gloucesters and 8th Worcester.	
"	19		Inspected animals at M.V.S. also S.A.A Section D.A.C. at LE FESTEL	G.O.M.
"	20		Visited 106th Field Coy R.E. en route for M.V.S.	G.O.M.
			Visited and made arrangements for fresh card for M.V.S at ST	
			RIQUIER. Visited 8th Warwicks.	G.O.M.
"	21		Visited 9th Yorks, 11th Notts Derbys and 13th Durham L.I.	G.O.M.
"	22		Visited 75th Field Amb, 201 Coy A.S.C. and 74th Bde I.H.R.	G.O.M.
"	23		Inspected 105th 3rd Coy R.E. and 8th Warwicks. Visited	G.O.M.
			M.V.S. and inspected animals for evacuation.	G.O.M.
"	24		Inspected 200 Coy A.S.C., 106th Field Coy R.E. and 20th and 21st	
			Manchesters	G.O.M.

Army Form C. 2118.

WAR DIARY
or
INTELLIGENCE SUMMARY.

(Erase heading not required.)

Instructions regarding War Diaries and Intelligence Summaries are contained in F. S. Regs., Part II. and the Staff Manual respectively. Title pages will be prepared in manuscript.

(2)

Place	Date Sept 1918	Hour	Summary of Events and Information	Remarks and references to Appendices
ST ROUIER	26		Units commenced moving to new area.	G.O.N.
HENENCOURT	27		D.H.Q. moved to HENENCOURT.	G.O.N.
"	28		Visited M.V.S. and inspected camp etc. Visited 106 Field Coy R.E. and 75 Inf. Bde.	E.O.N.
MONTAUBAN	29		D.H.Q. moved to MONTAUBAN.	E.O.N.
"	30		Inspected animals and camp of M.V.S.	E.O.N.

Vol 38

War Diary
of
Major G.D. Norman, A.V.C.
"D.A.D.V.S. 25th Division"
for Month of October 1918
Volume XXXVII

Army Form C. 2118.

WAR DIARY
or
INTELLIGENCE SUMMARY.

(Erase heading not required.)

Instructions regarding War Diaries and Intelligence Summaries are contained in F. S. Regs., Part II. and the Staff Manual respectively. Title pages will be prepared in manuscript.

Place	Date	Hour	Summary of Events and Information	Remarks and references to Appendices

Army Form C. 2118.

WAR DIARY
or
INTELLIGENCE SUMMARY.
(Erase heading not required.)

Instructions regarding War Diaries and Intelligence Summaries are contained in F.S. Regs., Part II. and the Staff Manual respectively. Title pages will be prepared in manuscript.

Place	Date Oct 1918	Hour	Summary of Events and Information	Remarks and references to Appendices
COMBLES	1		D.H.Q. moved from MONTAUBAN to COMBLES.	A.D.M.
"	2		Visited horses of D.H.Q. and M.V.S. Inspected 75th Inf. Bde.	A.D.M.
NURLU	3		D.H.Q. moved to NURLU. Inspected 130th Field Coy RE	A.D.M.
ST EMILIE	4		D.H.Q. moved to ST EMILIE. Inspected M.V.S, 200 and 201 Coys ASC	A.D.M.
"	5		Inspected 75th Inf. Bde, 75 and 77 Field Amb.	A.D.M.
TEMPLEUX	6		D.H.Q moved to TEMPLEUX LE GUERRARD. Inspected 105 Field Coy RE	A.D.M.
"	7		and 7th and Two 17th Sections D.A.C. Inspected animals for evacuation at M.V.S, also inspected M.G. Battn at ST EMILIE. 198 Coy ASC	A.D.M.
BELLICOURT	8		D.H.Q. moved to BELLICOURT.	A.D.M.
PONCHAUX	9		D.H.Q moved to PONCHAUX. Visited J.H.Q., Signals and 130th Field Coy RE	A.D.M.
LES TROUX aux SOLDATS	10		D.H.Q moved to LES TROUX AUX SOLDATS	A.D.M.
"	11		Inspected transport of 7th Inf. Bde, 77th Field Amb. and 75th Field Amb.; also visited M.V.S and examined animals in camp	A.D.M.
SERAIN	12		D.H.Q moved to SERAIN.	A.D.M.

WAR DIARY
or
INTELLIGENCE SUMMARY.

(Erase heading not required.)

Army Form C. 2118.

Place	Date	Hour	Summary of Events and Information	Remarks and references to Appendices
SERAIN	Oct 13		Visited Q.R. Reserve and 20th & 21st Manchesters, also inspected 75th Inf. Bde with exception of S.R. Worcester.	F.M.
"	14		Inspected 1st Section D.A.C. and 110th Bde R.F.A.	F.M.
"	15		Inspected 11th South Lancs (Pioneers), 105th Field By R.E. and 11th Notts & Derbys. Visited Northumberland Hussars.	F.M.
"	16		Visited inspected 46 remounts at Refilling Point, also visited M.V.S. and examined animals for evacuation to.	F.M.
"	17		Visited A.D.V.S. XIII Corps also inspected horses of No. 2. Dufflic. Control at LE CATELET. D.H.Q. starting 6" in afternoon.	F.M.
"	18		Inspected 77th Field Amb. and 74th Inf. Bde, also visited M.V.S. and inspected animals for evacuation. D.H.Q. moved to HONNECHY.	F.M.
HONNECHY	19		Inspected 165 & 176 Field Coys R.E.	F.M.
"	20		Visited M.V.S. at MARETZ inspected animals for evacuation Inspected 75th Field Amb. and 11th Notts and Derbys.	F.M.
"	21		Visited 112th Bde R.F.A. and 25 Bn M.G.C.	F.M.

WAR DIARY
or
INTELLIGENCE SUMMARY.

(Erase heading not required.)

Army Form C. 2118.

Place	Date	Hour	Summary of Events and Information	Remarks and references to Appendices
	Oct 1918			
HONNECHY	22		Visited M.V.S. and inspected animals and camp. Inspected 76th Field Amb, 179th & 200 Cos A.S.C.	F.M.
LE CATEAU	23		D.H.Q. moved to LE CATEAU. Inspected J.H.Q. Signals	F.M.
	24		Inspected 112th Bde R.F.A and 77th Field Amb	F.M.
	25		Visited M.V.S. and inspected animals for evacuation, also 195 and 201 Cos A.S.C. Visited transport of 7th Inf Bde and 106th Field Coy R.E.	F.M.
"	26		Visited M.V.S. and Nos 1 & 2 Sections D.A.C.; also inspected 112 Bde R.F.A.	F.M.
"	27		Visited inspected 110 & 111 Bde R.F.A, 130 Field Coy R.E., animals at M.V.S.	F.M.
"	28		Inspected 75th Inf Bde	F.M.
"	29		Inspected 165 Field Coy R.E. 76th Field Amb. Visited C.R.A.	F.M.
"	30		Visited A.D.V.S., XIII Corps and inspected M.V.S.	F.M.
"	31		Visited and inspected transport of 7th Inf Bde and H.Q. A.D.V.S., XIII Corps. Signals, also visited A.D.V.S., XIII Corps	F.M.

Joined B.E.F. 25.9.1915

Vol 39

Confidential

War Diary

of

Major G.D. Turner, A.V.C.,

D.A.D.V.S., 25th Division

for month of

November

1916

WAR DIARY
or
INTELLIGENCE SUMMARY.
(Erase heading not required.)

Army Form C. 2118.

Place	Date 1915	Hour	Summary of Events and Information	Remarks and references to Appendices
LE CATEAU	Nov. 1		Visited 110th Bde R.F.A. inspected same also 77th Field Amb.	E.M.
"	2		Inspected 112th Bde. R.F.A. M.V.S. and animals for evacuation also 7th	E.M.
			Inf. Bde.	
"	3		Visited POMMEREUIL manager position for Advanced T&H Park.	
			Inspected transport equipment of 75th Inf. Bde.	E.M.
"	4		Visited Advnd T&H Park also M.V.S. Visited 7th Inf. Bde.	E.M.
"	5		Visited POMMEREUIL reinspected area at Advnd T&H Park re M.V.S.	E.M.
LANDRECIES	6		D.H.Q. moved to LANDRECIES. Selected camp for M.V.S.	E.M.
"	7		Inspected M.V.S. camp &c. Visited 75 & Field Amb. H&S Sec A.V.R.E.	E.M.
"	8		Visited S.A.A. Section D.A.C. 199, 200 & 201 Coy A.S.C.	E.M.
"	9		Inspected 110th & 112th Bde R.F.A. on the march also 75th Inf. Bde and	
			76th Field Amb.	
"	10		Inspected camp of M.V.S. also 7th Inf. Bde.	E.M.
"	11		Visited 110th Bde R.F.A. re Outbreak of ringworm. Also 74th Inf. Bde.	E.M.
"	12		Inspected No 112 Section D.A.C. also M.V.S.	E.M.
LE CATEAU	13		D.H.Q. moved from LANDRECIES to LE CATEAU.	E.M.

Army Form C. 2118.

WAR DIARY
or
INTELLIGENCE SUMMARY.
(Erase heading not required.)

Instructions regarding War Diaries and Intelligence Summaries are contained in F. S. Regs., Part II. and the Staff Manual respectively. Title pages will be prepared in manuscript.

Place	Date Nov 1918	Hour	Summary of Events and Information	Remarks and references to Appendices
LE CATEAU	14		Inspected 7th Inf Bde also 110th 112th & 121st Bde RFA on the march. Inspected animals for evacuation at MVS.	E.M.
"	15		Visited 199 Coy ASC and inspected 46 remounts for distribution.	E.M.
"	16		Inspected 77th Field Amb.	E.M.
"	17		Visited ADVS, XIII Corps and inspected SAA Section DAC.	E.M.
"	18		Inspected camp of MVS, also animals for evacuation.	E.M.
"	19		Inspected animals returning equipment of 110 ABde RFA.	E.M.
"	20		Inspected 110th Bde RFA also animals for evacuation in MVS.	E.M.
"	21		Inspected 112 Bde RFA and 77th Field Amb.	E.M.
"	22		Inspected transport of 115th Gloucesters & 8th Worcesters. 1st Bn Coy ASC. Inspected 118th Warwicks & 11th 75th Inf Bde: also visited No 3 Section DAC.	E.M.
"	23		Inspected animals for evacuation at MVS also 75th Field Amb.	E.M.
"	24		Visited ADVS XIII Corps.	E.M.
"	25		Visited 199, 199 & 200 Coys ASC.	E.M.
"			Visited 165 HQ Coy RE, MVS, and ADVS XIII Corps.	E.M.

Army Form C. 2118.

WAR DIARY
or
INTELLIGENCE SUMMARY.
(Erase heading not required.)

(3)

Place	Date	Hour	Summary of Events and Information	Remarks and references to Appendices
LE CATEAU	Nov 1918 26		Inspected 76th Field Amb, 7th & 15th also camp equipment of M.V.S.	G.M.
"	27		Inspected 25 Br. M.G.C. and 11th Scott Force (Pioneers)	G.M.
"	28		Visited BOUSSIERES to find camp for M.S. Inspected 130th Field Amb.	G.M.
"	29		Visited AVESNES in M.V.	G.M.
AVESNES LEZ AUBERT	30		D.H.Q. moved to AVESNES LEZ AUBERT	G.M.

Joined B.E.F. 26-9-1915

VOL 40

Confidential

War Diary

of

D.A.D.V.S., 25th Division.

for Month of

December

1914

Volume XXXIX

Army Form C. 2118.

WAR DIARY
or
INTELLIGENCE SUMMARY.
(Erase heading not required.)

Instructions regarding War Diaries and Intelligence Summaries are contained in F. S. Regs., Part II. and the Staff Manual respectively. Title pages will be prepared in manuscript.

Place	Date	Hour	Summary of Events and Information	Remarks and references to Appendices

(A9375) Wt W3538/P350 600,000 12/17 D. D. & L. **Sch. 52a.** Forms/C.2118/15.

Army Form C. 2118.

WAR DIARY
or
INTELLIGENCE SUMMARY.
(Erase heading not required.)

Place	Date	Hour	Summary of Events and Information	Remarks and references to Appendices
	DECEMBER 1918.			
AVESNES-LEZ-	1		Inspected 75th Field Amb.	G.M.
AUBERT	2		Inspected 76th Field Amb. and 112th Bde R.F.A.	G.M.
"	3		Inspected 110th Bde R.F.A. and animals for promotion at M.V.S.	G.M.
			Also tore in Segregation Camp.	
"	4		Inspected 7th Inf Bde and 77th Field Amb.	G.M.
"	5		Inspected 105 Fd Coy R.E, 199 Coy R.A.S.C & 76th Field Amb.	G.M.
"	6		Visited M.V.S, M.G. Batt., and "C" Batty, 110th Bde R.F.A	G.M.
"	7		Visited 76th Field Amb. and 112th Bde R.F.A.	G.M.
"	8		Inspected 75th Inf Bde	G.M.
"	9		Visited and accompanied A.D.V.S. XIII Corps in his inspection	G.M.
			of 110th Bde R.F.A	
"	10		Visited and accompanied A.D.V.S. XIII Corps in his inspection	G.M.
			of D.A.C. 7th Inf Bde and 77th Field Amb.	
"	11		Visited Winners 105 R. Field CyRE and M.V.S	G.M.
"	12		Visited M.O. Signals and animals of D.H.Q.	G.M.
"	13		Visited 112th Bde R.F.A and 76th Field Amb.	G.M.

WAR DIARY
or
INTELLIGENCE SUMMARY.
(Erase heading not required.)

Army Form C. 2118.

Place	Date	Hour	Summary of Events and Information	Remarks and references to Appendices
	DECEMBER 1916			
AVESNES LEZ ALBERT	14		Inspected 75th Inf Bde and 130 3rd Cy RE	E.M.
	15		Visited No 1 Section DAC also Pioneers.	E.M.
"	16		Examined foot march of 112th Bde RFA with Corps Farrier	E.M.
"	17		Inspected foot march mounted at DHQ and visited CAMBRAI	E.M.
			6 remaining teams of 75th Inf Bde Group.	
"	18		Visited MVS and inspected animal camp. Visited	E.M.
			200 Cy RASC and 130 3rd Cy RE.	
"	19		Visited 74th Inf Bde, also 106 3rd Cy RE.	E.M.
"	20		Visited MVS. Examined ADVS XIII Corps & selection	E.M.
			of good mules.	
"	21		Inspected A, B and D Batteries of 110th Bde, also 77th Field Amb	E.M.
"	22		Inspected cart of MVS, also 200 Cy RASC.	E.M.
"	23		Visited JHQ, DAC and Nos 2 & 3 Sections.	E.M.
"	24		Visited 7th Inf Bde & 130 3rd Cy RE.	E.M.
"	25		Visited MVS & C. Batty 110th Bde.	E.M.
"	26		Inspected Pioneers and Signal Coy.	E.M.

WAR DIARY
or
INTELLIGENCE SUMMARY.

Army Form C. 2118.

Place	Date	Hour	Summary of Events and Information	Remarks and references to Appendices
	DECEMBER 1918.			
MESNES LES HUBERT	27		Visited M.G. Batt. and 165 Field Coy. R.E.	G.M.
	28		Scanned arrivals of D.H.Q., M.M.P., H.Q. Signals and J.H.Q. Train clearing same	
	29		Visited M.V.S. and 102 Section D.A.C.	G.M.
	30		Visited CAMBRAI examining mined # 75th # Rl.Guard clearing same	G.M. G.M.
	31		Visited RIEUX examining M.G. Batt. and C/Batty 110 R. Bde mines and clearing same	G.M.

4 25

Vol 41

CONFIDENTIAL.

WAR DIARY.

OF

MAJOR G. D. NORMAN. R.A.V.C.

D.A.D.V.S. 25TH DIVISION.

FOR MONTH OF JANUARY.

1919.

VOLUME XL

DUPLICATE.

WAR DIARY
or
INTELLIGENCE SUMMARY.
(Erase heading not required.)

Army Form C. 2118.

Place	Date	Hour	Summary of Events and Information	Remarks and references to Appendices
AYSSNES LEZ AUBERT.	JANUARY 1919.			
	1.		Inspected animals of 74th Inf. Bde. Group and classifying same.	E.O.M.
	2.		Inspected animals of 75th Field Ambce, R.A.H.Q. & R.E. H.Q's	E.O.M.
	3.		Visited 74" Inf. Bde. Group and classifying animals.	E.O.M.
	4.		Inspected animals 196 Coy. R.A.S.C., 9th Batt. Yorks and 11 Bn. South Lancs Regt.	E.O.M.
	5.		Visited and classifying animals S.A.A. Section 25th D.A.C.	E.O.M.
	6.		Inspecting and classifying animals of B/110 = D/110 Bdes. R.F.A., including H.Q's of 110 Bde. R.F.A.	E.O.M.
	7.		Inspecting and classifying animals No. 1 Section - No. 2 Section 25th D.A.C.	E.O.M.
	8.		Visited CARNIERES and classifying animals H.Q's 112th Bde. R.F.A. and A/112 also B/112.	E.O.M.
	9.		Visited CARNIERES inspecting animals 112" Bde. R.F.A. Inspected 37th hostile Veterinary Section.	E.O.M.
	10		Inspecting animals of 25th Machine Gun Battalion and classifying animals of C/112 = D/112 Bde. R.F.A.	E.O.M.
	11		Visited NEUVILLE and classified animals A/110 Bde. R.F.A.	E.O.M.

Army Form C. 2118.

WAR DIARY
or
INTELLIGENCE SUMMARY.
(Erase heading not required.)

Place	Date	Hour	Summary of Events and Information	Remarks and references to Appendices
	December 1919.			
AVESNES LEZ AUBERT.	12.		Visited CAMBRAI for reclassification of animals of 200 Coy. R.A.S.C., 130th Coy. R.E. and 76th Field Ambulance.	G.M.
	13.		Reclassification of animals of 198 Coy R.A.S.C. Visited A.D.V.S. at H.Q. XVIII Corps.	G.M.
	14.		Visited CARNIERES, re classifying, also ROMERIES and inspected 199 Coy R.A.S.C.	G.M.
	15.		Attended Court of Enquiry re death of animals in R.A.S.C.	G.M.
	16.		Visited and classifying animals 201 Coy R.A.S.C. Inspected 37th Mob. Vet'y Section.	G.M.
	17.		Visited 14th Army Aux (H) Coy at SOLESMES + classified animals of same, also 6th Canadian Railway Troops at AULNOYE.	G.M.
	18.		Visited and classified animals 7th Canadian R.T. at SOLESMES.	G.M.
	19.		Visited CAMBRAI + ST. HILAIRE, re classification of animals.	G.M.
	20.		Attended Court of Enquiry re death of A.S.C. animals at SALESCHES.	G.M.
	21.		Visited 198 Coy R.A.S.C. completed classification of animals. Inspected 37 Mob V.S.	G.M.
	22.		Inspected animals 7th Can. R.T. before their leaving area, and visited 110th Bde. R.F.A. re outbreak of Mange.	G.M.
	23.		Visited 37th M.V.S., and drew meat animals for sale to butchers also those in segregation.	G.M.

Army Form C. 2118.

WAR DIARY
or
INTELLIGENCE SUMMARY.
(Erase heading not required.)

(3)

Place	Date	Hour	Summary of Events and Information	Remarks and references to Appendices
	JANUARY 1919			
AVESNES LEZ AUBERT.	24		Visited CARNIERES inspected animals 112 Bde. R.F.A. Inspected animals of 11 Bn. Scottish Lancs. Regt. at SOLESMES.	G.W.M.
	25		Visited BEAUVOIS and inspected Staying Camp, making arrangements for same. Veterinary Infirmary	G.W.M.
	26		Visited ST HILAIRE to see V.O. and inspected "Y" animals being demobilized.	E.D.M.
	27		Taking over charge of 37" Mot. Vety Section during absence of V.O. 4/c.	E.D.M.
	28		Visited A.D.V.S. XIII Corps and Staging Camp at BEAUVOIS.	E.D.M.
	29		Duties at 37" Mot. Vety. Section	E.D.M.
	30		Duties at 37" Mot. Vety. Section and mallein work.	E.D.M.
	31		Duties at 37" Mot. Vety. Section and visiting units re mallein tests.	E.D.M.

WAR DIARY

OF

MAJOR G.D. NORMAN. R.A.V.C.

D.A.D.V.S. 25" Division

FOR THE

MONTH OF FEBRUARY

1919.

VOL. XL

WAR DIARY
INTELLIGENCE SUMMARY

(Erase heading not required.)

Vol. XL

Army Form C. 2118.

Place	Date	Hour	Summary of Events and Information	Remarks and references to Appendices
	FEBRUARY 1919			
AVESNES LEZ AUBERT	1.		Duty at 37th M.V.S. Mustering animals in 73rd Field Ambulance and H.Q. Signals	G.O.R.
"	2.		Duty at 37th M.V.S. and inspecting animals returning	G.O.R.
"	3.		Duty at 37th M.V.S. and inspecting animals for demobilisation	G.O.R.
"	4.		Duty at 37th M.V.S. Mustering and inspecting animals for demobilisation	G.O.R.
"	5.		Duty at 37th M.V.S. Mustering animals of H.Q. Signals	G.O.R.
"	6.		Duty at 37th M.V.S. Visited 110th Bde. R.F.A.	G.O.R.
"	7.		Duty at 37th M.V.S. Visited Animal Collecting Camp at BEAUVOIS	G.O.R.
"	8.		Duty at 37th M.V.S. Visited 198 Coy 25th Div. Train and A.D.V.S. XIII Corps.	G.O.R.
"	9.		Duty at 37th M.V.S. Visited work at CAMBRAI	G.O.R.
"	10		Duty at 37th M.V.S. Visited H.Q. 25th Div. Train	G.O.R.
"	11		Duty at 37th M.V.S. Major G.D. NORMAN proceeded on leave 15 U.K. Capt. I.H. JONES	G.O.R.
"			O.C. 37th M.V.S. appointed acting D.A.D.V.S. 25th Division.	J.H.J.
"	12.		Duty at 37th M.V.S. Arranging for sale by auction of "Z" animals	J.H.J.
"	13		Duty at 37th M.V.S. Arranging for sale at SOLESMES on 15/2/19 of "Z" animals	J.H.J.
"	14		Duty at 37th M.V.S. Arranging parade at SOLESMES on 15/2/19 of "Z" animals	J.H.J.
"	15		Sale of 111 "Z" animals by auction at SOLESMES.	J.H.J.

Army Form C. 2118.

WAR DIARY
or
INTELLIGENCE SUMMARY.
(Erase heading not required.)

Instructions regarding War Diaries and Intelligence Summaries are contained in F.S. Regs., Part II. and the Staff Manual respectively. Title pages will be prepared in manuscript.

Place	Date	Hour	Summary of Events and Information	Remarks and references to Appendices
HUESNES LEZ AUBERT	FEBRUARY 1919 16.		Visited Field Cashier XVII Corps and paid in proceeds of Sale at SOLESMES 15/2/19	9H1
	17.		Arranging for Sale of "Z" animals at CAMBRAI on 18/2/19. Duty at "Z" M.V.S.	9H9
	18.		Sale of 75 "Z" animals by auction at CAMBRAI	9H9
	19.		Visited Field Cashier and paid in proceeds of Sale on 18/2/19. Arranging Sale for 20/2/19	9H9
	20.		Sale of 101 "Z" animals at SOLESMES by auction	9H9
	21.		Sale of 101 "Z" animals at CAMBRAI by auction	9H9
	22.		Visited Field Cashier and paid in proceeds of Sales on 20th and 21st	9H9
	23.		Arranging for Sales at SOLESMES on 24/2/19 and CAMBRAI 25/2/19	9H9
	24.		Sale of 103 "Z" animals at SOLESMES by auction	9H9
	25.		Sale of 100 "Z" animals at CAMBRAI by auction	9H9
	26.		Visited Field Cashier to pay in proceeds of Sales on 24th and 25th	9H9
	27.		Sale of 100 "Z" animals at SOLESMES by auction	9H9
	28		Visited Field Cashier to pay in proceeds of sale at SOLESMES	9H9

www.ingramcontent.com/pod-product-compliance
Lightning Source LLC
Chambersburg PA
CBHW081354160426
43192CB00013B/2409